Capital Controls:
A 'Cure' Worse than the Problem?

Capital Controls: A 'Cure' Worse than the Problem?

FORREST CAPIE

The Institute of Economic Affairs
in association with the Wincott Foundation

First published in Great Britain in 2002 by
The Institute of Economic Affairs
2 Lord North Street
Westminster
London SW1P 3LB
in association with Profile Books Ltd

A CIP catalogue record for this book is available from the British Library.

ISBN 0 255 36506 3

Many IEA publications are translated into languages other than English or are
reprinted. Permission to translate or to reprint should be sought from the
General Director at the address above.

Typeset in Stone by MacGuru
info@macguru.org.uk

Printed and bound in Great Britain by Hobbs the Printers

CONTENTS

ACKNOWLEDGEMENTS

This short study was both suggested and made possible by the Wincott Foundation. I am in their debt for their provision of financial support for the necessary research. I thank Mark Billings for research assistance and John Chown for making available to me papers on the subject of the abolition of exchange controls in Britain in 1979 that he wrote at the time. I thank Geoffrey Wood and Sir Geoffrey Owen for their valuable comments on a first draft of the manuscript, and two anonymous referees for helpful comments.

THE AUTHOR

Forrest Capie is Professor of Economic History at the City University Business School, London. He was Head of Department of Banking and Finance at the university from 1989 to 1992. He trained first as an accountant and worked as one before joining the Department of Trade and Industry in New Zealand. He then studied economics and economic history and, after a doctorate at the London School of Economics in the 1970s and a teaching fellowship there, taught at the Universities of Warwick and Leeds.

He has been a British Academy Overseas Fellow at the National Bureau, New York, and a Visiting Professor at the University of Aix-Marseille, and at the London School of Economics. He has written widely on money, banking, and trade and commercial policy. He was editor of the *Economic History Review* from 1993 to 1999, and is a member of the Council of the Economic History Society.

FOREWORD

The use of capital controls is one of those policies which always seems to lie just below the surface of economic discussion: at the first hint of a financial 'crisis', the idea is resurrected and, surprisingly, is occasionally supported by economists who, in other respects, subscribe to liberal ideas. They may look on such controls as a 'temporary' measure, designed to give an economy some breathing space. Other supporters of controls on capital flows, for example in the anti-globalisation and anti-capitalism movements, seem to view controls as a more permanent feature of the world economy.

As Professor Forrest Capie shows in his fascinating account of the history of capital flows and capital controls since the latter part of the nineteenth century, the idea of controlling capital movements is by no means new. In the nineteenth century, the forces of integration were similarly resisted. But, he argues, free flows of capital are a powerful force for economic development: capital controls strike at the roots of these flows. Even in emergency, it is difficult to see what useful purpose controls can serve. Moreover, like all protectionist measures, once imposed, capital controls are difficult to remove because they attract a constituency that benefits from them and will resist abolition: the long period of exchange control in Britain (1939–79) is testament to the longevity of such forms of regulation.

Recommendations for controls on capital movements, says Professor Capie, are based on misdiagnosis of the issues. It is not the volatility of capital movements which is the problem. It is 'defective domestic banking systems and poorly conceived exchange-rate regimes' which are at fault. He examines instances of the imposition of capital controls over the years, including the British experience and the recent return of capital controls in Chile and in the Far East during the late 1990s, as well as the theory relating to capital movements. His detailed examination of history and theory leads him to conclude that 'The history of the last 150 years lends strong support to the case for freedom.' Capital controls impose 'deadweight losses' on the economy through the distortions they cause, damage the credibility of the government's commitment to a market economy, and are redundant if a proper exchange-rate regime is in place: 'there is no such thing as a bad capital movement, only bad exchange-rate systems'.

As with all IEA publications, the views expressed in this Research Monograph are those of the author, not those of the Institute (which has no corporate view), its managing trustees, Academic Advisory Council members or senior staff. But Professor Capie's powerful case for freedom of capital movements, based on his detailed analysis of economic history, is one that should be heeded by all those who flirt with the idea of imposing controls, temporary or otherwise, on those flows of capital which nourish the economic development of both poor and rich countries.

COLIN ROBINSON

Editorial Director, Institute of Economic Affairs

Professor of Economics, University of Surrey

May 2002

SUMMARY

- Capital controls have a long history: some economists have recently begun to advocate their revival. The anti-globalisation and anti-capitalist movements also support such controls.
- Under the gold standard there were no problems about exchange rates, the balance of payments or inflation for 'well-behaved countries'. But the gold standard was not fully restored after World War I. The economic problems of the inter-war years were thought to be due partly to 'capital flight'.
- After World War II, the Bretton Woods system was established, with a tenuous link to gold, but its rules were never fully followed. By the 1970s the world had moved to fiat money for the first time.
- Capital flows, quite small early in the nineteenth century, were by the end of the century on a 'remarkable scale'.
- Before 1914 capital flows were around 4 per cent of GDP in the major world economies. By the 1930s they had diminished to 1.5 per cent of GDP. Their all-time low, in the 1960s, was 1 per cent of GDP. Even in the 1980s and 1990s, they were only 2–2.5 per cent of GDP – relatively much smaller than before World War I.
- The liberal order of the nineteenth century saw increasing

integration and globalisation, but these trends were reversed in the first half of the twentieth century. Not until the 1950s did the world economy begin to grow rapidly again.

- The modern use of capital controls dates back to the 1930s, when they were widely employed. Often they were imposed in times of 'crisis', but they long outlived the original crises.

- In theory, capital mobility improves the allocation of resources worldwide, channelling resources to their most productive uses. The presence of market 'imperfections' may appear to detract from these theoretical arguments, but there are enormous obstacles in the way of improving the market outcome by using capital controls.

- Analysis of British and other experience with capital controls shows that they result in 'deadweight losses': prices are higher, quantities produced are lower and there are bureaucratic costs. The controls are difficult to remove and they damage the credibility of the government's commitment to a market economy.

- In peacetime, and with 'proper exchange-rate regimes', there is no case for capital controls. Problems arise when exchange rates are no longer credible. It is a myth that capital flows are destabilising: 'there is no such thing as a bad capital movement, only bad exchange-rate systems'.

TABLES AND FIGURES

1   INTRODUCTION

The extent of the control over all life that economic control confers is nowhere better illustrated than in the field of foreign exchanges. Nothing would at first seem to affect private life less than a state control of the dealings in foreign exchange, and most people will regard its introduction with complete indifference. Yet the experience of most continental countries has taught thoughtful people to regard this step as the decisive advance on the path to totalitarianism and the suppression of individual liberty. It is in fact the complete delivery of the individual to the tyranny of the state, the final suppression of all means of escape – not merely for the rich but for everybody. Once the individual is no longer free to travel, no longer free to buy foreign books or journals, once all the means of foreign contact can be restricted to those of whom official opinion approves or for whom it is regarded as necessary, effective control of opinion is much greater than that ever exercised by any of the absolutist governments of the seventeenth and eighteenth centuries.

F. A. HAYEK, THE ROAD TO SERFDOM, P. 69

Despite these powerful words from Hayek, some economists still advocate such controls. This short study brings some historical perspective to the subject and argues that these proposals are a consequence of a misdiagnosis – as were similar proposals in the inter-war years.

In the last twenty years or so, the world has become increasingly dominated by market economies. Planning and state control have been rejected in favour of market solutions. In the market economies themselves there have been ever-spreading deregulation of markets and a retreat by governments from activities formerly believed to be more appropriately carried out by them. Where once market failure was found to be extensive, there came a point when it was recognised that market failure was less serious than the government failure that came to replace it.

This process can be seen as part of a much longer process of liberalisation in international trade and in domestic economies which could be dated from the end of World War II. A case could easily be made for dating it from much earlier – somewhere in the nineteenth century – and regarding the inter-war years as an interruption to the process of globalisation. Globalisation is certainly not new. It might even be argued that the process of increasing integration in the world economy has in one sense been going on since the beginning of time. But it was really with the coming of the British liberal order in the nineteenth century, following two centuries or more of mercantilism, that globalisation accelerated. In the second half of the nineteenth century international trade grew quickly, capital flows reached a colossal scale and labour migrated mainly from the old world to the new in tens of millions. This process was interrupted with the outbreak of war in 1914, and it did not begin to get back on track until after World War II. Then the process began to shake off the controls born in war and depression and speeded up in the 1980s and 1990s. Yet the world economy of the late nineteenth century may well have been more integrated than that of the late twentieth century.

At the same time as the recent liberalisation has been spreading, there has been a growing swell of popular resistance to the forces of integration. Globalisation fills some with hope and others with gloom. For some it is a blessing and for others a curse. It is the resisters who have been claiming much of the attention recently. Thus, for example, a certain anti-capitalist strain and another distinct anti-free-trade strand were seen at the World Trade Organisation (WTO) talks in Seattle in November 1999 and in the opposition to the International Monetary Fund (IMF) meetings in Washington in April 2000. Much of the resistance was confused. There is also often an expression of underlying distrust of multinational companies and a suspicion about a supposed sinister role they play in influencing the whole process. However, there is at the same time a more general and sometimes wholly respectable source of doubters. For example, in December 1999 Michel Camdessus, then Managing Director of the IMF, felt it necessary to say, 'The globalisation of financial markets – while it has benefited global growth, especially in the longer term – has contributed in recent years to several crises . . . ' (Camdessus, 1999). It has not been uncommon to identify these recent interruptions to the process of rapid integration as evidence of major flaws in the system. The stumbling of the 'Asian tigers' and some other countries in the late 1990s gave some cause for concern. But although the danger appeared to have passed as early as late 1999 there were many calls for controls, including capital controls. There were similar forces of resistance in the late nineteenth century, resisting the trends to integration.

When the world economy was undergoing rapid change in the closing years of the twentieth century it was not surprising that there were some bumpy periods, and that different countries experienced different problems. A great deal has been written about the weakness of certain systems and the fragility of particular regimes, and a variety of solutions proposed. Should there be fixed, pegged, or floating exchange-rate regimes, monetary unions or currency boards? Might there be international supervision and regulation of financial markets, deposit insurance, international bankruptcy courts, an international lender of last resort or capital controls, or some combination of some of these? Many leading economists have advocated some of these 'solutions'. This paper concentrates on only one of the many strands in the process – capital flows and capital controls – and tries to disentangle these from the other issues, and consider the case for freedom from controls.

The conclusions of the paper can be stated briefly. Free capital flows are a powerful force for economic development. Capital controls are damaging. That much is clear from economic theory. Indeed, it is difficult to see what case can be made for capital controls. Even the argument that they can be useful in an emergency is difficult to sustain, with the exception of wartime. One practical problem is that, once imposed, like all protectionist measures, they become difficult to remove. They are often extended and finish up being redundant or harmful, as the 'time inconsistency' literature in economics would predict. Further, controls damage the market environment. Once imposed, they affect the credibility of the government's policy stance. The danger is that what might appear as a one-off policy action could alert the market to the possibility of a repeat. The history of the last 150 years lends strong support to the case for freedom.

Perhaps the most serious point to make is that recent recommendations for capital controls are simply misdirected because of misdiagnosis of the problem. The problems do not lie in the volatility of capital movements but rather in defective domestic banking systems and poorly conceived exchange-rate regimes. Capital flight does not take place where there is belief in the soundness of the banking systems, belief in prudent monetary and fiscal policies, and where there are credible fixed exchange rates or freely floating rates in place.

The present paper first sets out the development of the international monetary system since the nineteenth century and the pattern of capital flows, and later controls, that arose. There follows some basic theory that allows a framework for discussion. An outline of the spread of controls is then given before a more detailed consideration of Britain's experience with controls; that is followed by some discussion of the recent return of controls in different parts of the world. Finally, following suggestions as to what the real problems and solutions are, some conclusions are drawn.

2 THE INTERNATIONAL MONETARY SYSTEM: AN OVERVIEW

Although money has existed in some form almost since the beginning of time, the same is not true of an international monetary system. The use of primitive money goes back to the earliest kind of exchange and can certainly be traced back to settled societies four thousand years ago. But that is different from a monetary economy, which is much more recent – dating back, say, to parts of medieval Europe. It could be argued that international monetary *relations* came some time after that, perhaps in the early modern period. But certainly there can be no discussion of an international monetary *system* (some set of rules more or less formally set out) until some time in the eighteenth or possibly even the nineteenth century. It was only after the spread of the nation state and national monies, and the growth of international trade itself, that such a system became possible.

Monetary systems evolved from the use of barter and primitive monies to systems based on metals. Precious metals were used for big transactions and common metals for day-to-day needs. It was the precious metals which mattered and came to define the system. Gold and silver came to predominate, sometimes as alternatives but sometimes as complements. They were the anchors of the system and prevented wild expansion of the money stock. There is some debate as to whether money evolved naturally in this way, with a weight of gold having a certain intrinsic monetary value, or whether it was the *imprimatur* of the nation's head of state on the coins that brought its value. Certainly heads of state were keen to see their image on coins and to benefit from the seigniorage. But either way there was a long period in the world's history when coins of different 'nationality' circulated freely in other countries. That was because their intrinsic value was known; they were declared legal tender of their home country, and they could be readily accepted for what they were worth.

In the course of the nineteenth century the gold standard was increasingly adopted – in part because Britain had adopted a gold standard, happened to be the first to industrialise and was immensely successful. The main alternatives were silver and bimetallic standards. To belong to the gold standard meant declaring a value for a currency (one ounce of gold as being equal to a certain unit of currency) and to allow the free export and import of gold. When several countries did this there was a system of fixed exchange rates in place, and it is then, in the nineteenth century, that there is an international monetary system in any meaningful sense.

The gold standard came to dominate and enjoyed its heyday in the period 1880–1914. It appeared to allow a wonderfully automatic means for holding prices together and adjusting balance of payments. Thus for well-behaved countries there were no problems about exchange rates, balance of payments or inflation. However, there is still great debate over how exactly the system worked. For example, did it need a strong hegemonic power such as Britain to orchestrate it? Did it need cooperating central banks to facilitate it? Was it the particular circumstances of the time and fortuitous capital flows which allowed it to function as smoothly as it did for most of its adherents?

Whatever the answer to these questions, the system came to at least a temporary halt on the outbreak of war in 1914. It was no longer sensible or feasible for major powers to allow the free export and import of gold. Thereafter, for the duration of the war and some time after, the world economy was highly disrupted, with governments free to issue money without constraint. Different countries then experienced different inflation rates. This, together with a shortage of gold, posed problems for the post-war economy. The nineteenth-century world of the gold standard was greatly desired in 1919, and the ambition to return to it was strong, but in the end it proved too difficult. A gold standard of a kind was restored, but it was one in which gold reserves had to be supplemented with foreign exchange. Although the basic sterling/dollar parity was restored, others were not.

Additionally, there were the major international problems of war debts, reparation payments, rising trade barriers, hyperinflation in central Europe and the accompanying capital flight. It is not difficult to appreciate the strains to which the system was subjected. The failure of the US Federal Reserve to act as it should (and could) have in the years 1928–32 initiated and then exacerbated the great depression. Britain abandoned the gold link in September 1931 when the world was in depression, and when the US did so in 1933 the system was effectively finished.

Throughout this long shaping of monetary systems there was a search for a means to ensure that money supply could be more elastic, yet sufficiently anchored to prevent undue expansion. In nineteenth-century Britain techniques were developed to meet these needs. In normal times the gold standard operated, but in times of danger – when liquidity was needed – the 1844 Bank Charter Act that defined the standard was suspended. This allowed an expansion of the fiduciary issue. Return to the requirements of the Act was effected quickly after the panic had subsided. When other countries joined the gold standard in the late nineteenth century, pressure was put on gold stocks. This stimulated discovery, but the question did arise as to how the system would work in future. After World War I there was the desire to return to a standard based on gold supplemented on the domestic level with fiat money, but at the international level it was to be supplemented with foreign exchange, hence the name gold-exchange standard. Clearly there was some advantage in having fiat money and foreign exchange, but what nevertheless frightened people was the sight of central and eastern Europe in the early 1920s awash with it, and suffering the inevitable hyperinflation. This created grave anxiety about the prospects for monetary stability.

It was this climate, together with the failure of the restored gold standard, compounded with the ineptitude of the Federal Reserve in the years 1928–32, which brought about and worsened the great depression in the US, which in turn had worldwide ramifications. The resulting mixture of dirty or managed exchange rates in the 1930s provoked a series of competitive devaluations – something future designers of the international monetary system would aim to avoid.

The problems of the inter-war years gave rise to different interpretations. There was the view that the fundamental problem of the time was inappropriate exchange rates. (See Haberler, 1939, for example.) The attempted restoration of the gold standard had depended on a variety of readings of price movements over the war years and after. Some countries aimed to select advantageous exchange rates. The principal alternative view was that the problem was capital flight. This was the view that developed in the

League of Nations in the 1930s and was expressed most clearly by Nurkse (1944). It was this view which dominated and became so influential in the design of the post-World War II system. From a modern perspective it looks odd, and needs explaining. The explanation can be found largely in historical circumstance. The impact of World War I was such that national security came to dominate in discussion, and national security played an important part in shaping exchange-rate regimes and financial regulation. (It continued to do so for a long period even after 1945.) The very phrase 'capital flight' carried the connotation of national betrayal (see James, 2003, for a development of these ideas).

This was the immediate background to discussions on an improved system. Two main proposals came from Britain (Keynes) and the US (Harry Dexter White). By the spring of 1944 the two proposals had been combined into the 'Joint Statement of Experts on the Establishment of an International Monetary Fund'. Keynes's scheme seemed to cover all international finance from post-war reconstruction through development finance, an investment board and so on. Of course, the British were keen to restore the position of sterling after the war to help Britain maintain its status as a leading power, but it was not at all clear that the US was supportive of this. The Keynes scheme would attend primarily to short-run balance-of-payments adjustment. The institution would issue a new international currency (the 'bancor') which would be held and used by central banks for settling the external account. The union would be there to provide liquidity with a view to keeping exchange rates stable. The plan was put forward in the midst of continuing Anglo-American talks on monetary and trade matters that ran throughout the war. The US, on the other hand, proposed (through White) a more limited stabilisation fund. (It is useful to recall that the US had established its own exchange stabilisation fund in 1934 to operate under the control of the Secretary of the Treasury.) White's plan was more conservative than Keynes's in that it saw the new institution's reserves being made up of national currencies and gold, rather than the institution having the power to create a new money.

Following several years of Anglo-American discussions, more than 300 representatives of 44 countries met in the small New Hampshire town of Bretton Woods in the summer of 1944. These meetings were to reach agreement on the details of the drafts submitted. The essence of the agreements was that the IMF would provide assistance to member countries to manage balance of payments in a way consistent with stable exchange rates, and would supply credit where needed. The principal obligation of members was to allow free convertibility for current account transactions – capital account controls were permitted. The IMF was established in 1945 and began operations in 1947. It had become apparent immediately that there was going to be a longer transition period than anticipated – the British were unsuccessful in their attempt (made under strong US pressure) to restore convertibility in 1947. Countries were therefore allowed a longer period in which to do this; the major industrial countries achieved it in 1958, but most countries did not and persisted with exchange controls until the 1990s.

So, in fact, a pegged-rate dollar standard emerged for the period 1950–70. For industrial countries other than the US this meant:

- a par value for the currency with the US dollar as *numeraire*, and keeping the exchange rate within 1 per cent of this value indefinitely;

- free currency convertibility for current account but use of capital controls, though the latter should be gradually freed;
- use of the US dollar as the intervention currency;
- subordination of long-run growth in domestic money supply to the exchange rate and US inflation rate; and
- limiting current account imbalances by using fiscal policy to offset imbalances between private saving and investment.

The US had to remain passive in the foreign exchanges, keep capital markets open, pursue an independent monetary policy and maintain its position as net creditor by limiting fiscal deficits. All this was clearly very different from the original intention.

The plan adopted was closer to White's plan than to Keynes's, but it inclined in some respects to the international clearing union in that it sought to avoid interference with domestic policies. The concentration was on developed industrial countries, and although the stabilisation fund had initially envisaged the new institution being a policeman with discretionary powers, it was to rely on the member countries behaving responsibly. Later that year it had developed into the Bretton Woods Agreements to establish the IMF and the World Bank.

Following the upheavals of the inter-war years the aims for the new international financial architecture of the time were to have stable and realistic exchange rates, with countries in difficulty having access to adequate international reserves to smooth out short-term problems. Good behaviour would be expected and some codes of behaviour put in place. This ambition in a way aimed to incorporate the good aspects of the past (the international gold standard of the nineteenth century) with the removal of the problems of the 1930s (restrictions and emphasis on domestic survival).

It has become increasingly recognised that the world never (or at best only for a very short time) followed the Bretton Woods rules. As Ronald McKinnon (1993: 601) has recently summarised it, the post-war monetary order envisaged by its designers had six main elements:

- fixing a foreign par value for domestic currency by using gold, or a currency linked to gold;
- keeping the exchange rate within 1 per cent of its par value in the short run;
- free currency convertibility for the current account but use of capital controls;
- use of national monies symmetrically in foreign transactions;
- drawing on official reserves and IMF credits for short-run payments imbalances and sterilising the domestic monetary impact of exchange market intervention; and
- each country to pursue its own price level and employment policies.

The rules were intended to apply to all nations equally, but as each country was to be free to pursue its own macroeconomic policies, it was recognised that this could result in differential inflation rates, hence the requirement for long-run flexibility in the exchange rate (the opposite of the pre-1914 gold standard).

However, although these had been the intentions, in fact the US emerged as the only country that could really behave autonomously, while 'other countries were caught in a strait-jacket – that is, a new and apparently unplanned international monetary standard – where the elbow room for exercising national macro autonomy was limited' (McKinnon, 1993: 602).

How did this change from the original intention come about? It might seem in some ways obvious that in wartime it would be very difficult to draw up a set of rules that could be applied in a post-war world that was impossible to envisage but was bound to be in some turmoil and more uncertain than usual. Feldstein (1993) says that instead of 'an arrangement in which exchange rates were determined in the market and national governments had responsibility for some domestic policies, the architects of the system created rules that appeared to be logically attractive but that were inapplicable in practice' (p. 615).

But following the spread of controls in the 1930s and the collapse of world trade, it was not surprising that stable exchange rates should be uppermost in designers' minds.

McKinnon (with others) argues that the Bretton Woods articles never came into effect, for something that was not anticipated was the impact of Marshall aid. One of the unknowns that were to materialise quite quickly at the end of the war was the extent of the threat of communism. (The Soviet Union had attended the Bretton Woods conference though it was unlikely to be a participant in the subsequent arrangements.) The urgency of containing communism was what prompted the US to support recovery programmes in many countries. Recovery in Europe and particularly in Germany was essential, and the US made extensive loans to European countries. When the worst harvest of the century and the most severe winter followed one another in 1946 and 1947, problems were worsened. In Europe reserves had been used and a desperate shortage of dollars and gold developed. It was here that Marshall aid came in. Without it there would have been a huge reduction in the extensive investment programmes which were designed to speed recovery and so contain the communist threat.

The argument in theory was that if a country balanced its budget and let its currency find its level in the market there would be no balance-of-payments 'problem'; there can be little argument with that, but the question is, at what cost in terms of output and employment? In normal times these might be pains that had to be borne, but in the context of the 1940s they had to be avoided 'at all costs'. What the plan provided was $13 billion over a period of three years for a speedy recovery programme – a mixture of grants, loans and conditional aid. Its importance for our purposes lies in how it changed the basis of the international monetary system.

Part of the recovery project was the establishment of the European Payments Union in 1950. This helped to restore current account convertibility in Europe, using the dollar as the unit of account for calculating credit balances. For the system to work, each country had to declare an exact dollar parity and then follow policies to keep this parity. This began in 1948 and was a means of trying to restore trade and financial stability in Europe. Mundell supports some of this story. He says that there never was a 'Bretton Woods system'. Instead the Bretton Woods Agreement 'accommodated the rest of the world to an international system that already existed' (1993: 605). He argues further, as others also had, that following the Tripartite Declaration of 1936, 'the essential structure of the gold–dollar standard was already determined' (ibid.) . When World War II broke out, European currencies became inconvertible, which strengthened the position of the dollar as the international means of settlement and standard of value.

All the immediate and more or less predictable difficulties consequent upon the end of the war, together with some exogenous and other unanticipated problems, meant it was impossible for the IMF to behave as planned. Pressnell (1997) maintains that the

IMF was 'effectively sidelined until the Suez crisis of 1956' (p. 214). The failure of sterling convertibility in 1947, the big French devaluation of 1948 (with multiple rates for hard currencies) and Italy's use of multiple rates, followed by Britain's devaluation of 1949, all damaged any prospect of the system working as intended, and the US granting of loans and then the Marshall Plan changed the nature of the system.

Following the period called Bretton Woods, where the link to gold had become even more tenuous, in the 1970s the world finally moved on to fiat money for the first time in its history. The 1970s and 1980s were characterised by inflation, and so the search continued for a new anchor, or as Redish (1993) puts it,

> ... as the inconsistency between discretionary monetary policy and 'anchoring' the money stock has become apparent, monetary authorities are searching for a new anchor: investing in reputations for low inflation; determining the optimal degree of independence for a central bank; choosing to form a currency union (p. 791).

3 CAPITAL FLOWS

The fundamental and favourable view of capital mobility is simply put. International capital markets let individuals pool various risks, allowing a better portfolio of assets than would otherwise be available. Similarly, a country that is in difficulties either from some unexpected disaster or from a downturn in economic activity can borrow on the international markets. When all the participants who wish to lend and borrow are left free to do so, world savings are channelled to their most productive uses. A slightly fuller examination of the theory is presented in a later section, but at least at this level the case for allowing or promoting capital mobility is a strong one.

In a world of such freedom policy-makers must be careful to avoid wild monetary and fiscal policies, for the participants will simply take their funds to safer havens – escape from inflation (bad for creditors) and concomitant depreciating exchange rates. There would be nothing speculative about such shifts, simply rational response to bad behaviour. The clear likelihood that this will happen should discipline governments.

Although it may be difficult to be precise about the benefits of capital flows, the unquantifiable benefits are likely to be substantial. The historical experience before the twentieth century certainly seems to have been a big success. If globalisation is taken to mean the ever-increasing integration of the world economy, then we can find the modern origins in the early eighteenth century. Larry Neal, in his book *The Rise of Financial Capitalism*, provides convincing evidence of an integrated capital market in the developed world in the early eighteenth century. There is certainly evidence of quite substantial capital flows in Europe in the course of the eighteenth century – mainly to do with the financing of war (Wright, 1997).

Capital flows, in what might be thought a modern form, were still quite small in the early nineteenth century by comparison with the end of the century. In the intervening years they picked up with increasing rapidity and reached a remarkable scale on the eve of the outbreak of World War I. The half-century from 1865 to 1914 was striking for the size and spread of capital flows around the world.

Given the nature of the data, it is difficult to reach agreement on the precise measure of these nineteenth-century capital flows. However, there can be little disagreement over the general orders of magnitude. By 1914 there was around £10 billion (roughly US$50 billion) of foreign investment. The principal holders of those assets were Britain and France, with 43 per cent and 20 per cent respectively. Germany had around 13 per cent and Belgium, Sweden and the Netherlands together 12 per cent. The US had been a substantial capital importer in the course of the nineteenth century but late in the century it had turned creditor and by 1914 held about 7 per cent of this total. The principal importers of capital were greater Europe and North America, with 27 per cent and 24 per cent respectively. Latin America followed with 19 per cent, then Asia (16 per cent), Africa (9 per cent) and Oceania (5 per cent).

Neither is it easy to find an acceptable multiplier to show what that US$50 billion of assets would be equivalent to today. However, some illustration can be given using the UK, for which there are measurably good data. Britain was the largest creditor by some distance and in the years immediately before 1914 was exporting annually something close to 10 per cent of GDP. (Britain had never at any time invested that kind of percentage domestically.) By 1914 Britain was holding close to £4,000 million of foreign assets, equal to roughly twice its GDP. In the early 1990s Japan was generally reckoned to be the world's greatest creditor, and many were inclined to say that Japan was the greatest creditor of all time. However, Japan held a much lower proportion of foreign assets to GDP than did Britain at its peak.

It is sometimes either assumed or asserted that nineteenth-century borrowing was all being done by governments, but this is not the case. Foreign government loans issues over the period 1870–1913 totalled £2.1 billion ($10.5 billion) or just a fifth of the total (Suzuki, 1993). The US was a large member of this group with £0.35 billion ($1.65 billion), about a seventh of the total. But, as would be expected, most countries feature at different points during the period. In terms of share of GDP, Canada emerges as the biggest importer, with 12 per cent in 1910. The most the US reached was around 3 per cent in 1870, and Sweden had 4 per cent in 1889.

Capital flows are usually divided into long-term and short-term. There are, as might be expected, some difficulties in distinguishing one from the other; indeed, for most purposes it proves impossible. Long-term flows are usually differentiated from short-term flows by the type of instrument. Long-term ones are usually thought of as new issues or transactions in bonds and equities, together with direct investment. But, of course, the sale and purchase of securities can and often does take place in very short periods, and against that short maturities (bills and the like) can be rolled over and so become a long-term investment. The other problem is to try to separate gross from net flows. Gross flows are all the transactions that take place; net flows capture the fundamental amounts.

The scale of capital flows is sometimes illustrated by quoting the average daily foreign exchange transactions in a particular market. So, for example, in 1973 foreign exchange trading was between $10 billion and $20 billion. By 1980 this had risen to an average of $80 billion, by 1992 to $880 billion, and in 1995 it reached $1,260 billion according to the Bank for International Settlements (BIS). The latest estimate is $3 trillion, of which one-third is carried out in London. Although this is interesting, it is not really an indication of what we are concerned with. Most of these transactions last for very short periods; investors keep responding to information and try to hold currencies they regard as somewhat below an anticipated value, and go short on those they believe are about to slip. In other words, there is a big difference between gross capital flows and net flows. It is net flows which really matter for the economy.

There have been three principal and rather obvious epochs in modern world financial history, and the flows of capital across borders coincide at least in broad terms with these epochs. The three periods are 1870–1914; the inter-war years; and the period after World War II.

An indication of the changing scale of capital flows across these periods is provided in the tables and graphs that follow. Obstfeld and Taylor's estimates are reproduced in Table 1. They have data on twelve important economies which made up the great bulk of world output, for the period 1870–1996. Their approach is

Table 1 The extent of capital flows since 1870. Mean absolute value of current account, 12 countries, selected periods. Percentage of GDP

	ARG	AUS	CAN	DEN	FRA	GER	ITA	JPN	NOR	SWE	GBR	USA	All
1870–1889	18.7	8.2	7.0	1.9	2.4	1.7	1.2	0.6	1.6	3.2	4.6	0.7	3.7
1890–1913	6.2	4.1	7.0	2.9	1.3	1.5	1.8	2.4	4.2	2.3	4.6	1.0	3.3
1914–1918	2.7	3.4	3.6	5.1	–	–	11.6	6.8	3.8	6.5	3.1	4.1	(5.1)
1919–1926	4.9	4.2	2.5	1.2	2.8	2.4	4.2	2.1	4.9	2.0	2.7	1.7	3.1
1927–1931	3.7	5.9	2.7	0.7	1.4	2.0	1.5	0.6	2.0	1.8	1.9	0.7	2.1
1932–1939	1.6	1.7	2.6	0.8	1.0	0.6	0.7	1.0	1.1	1.5	1.1	0.4	1.2
1940–1946	4.8	3.5	3.3	2.3	–	–	3.4	1.0	4.9	2.0	7.2	1.1	(3.2)
1947–1959	2.3	3.4	2.3	1.4	1.5	2.0	1.4	1.3	3.1	1.1	1.2	0.6	1.8
1960–1973	1.0	2.3	1.2	1.9	0.6	1.0	2.1	1.0	2.4	0.7	0.8	0.5	1.3
1974–1989	1.9	3.6	1.7	3.2	0.8	2.1	1.3	1.8	5.2	1.5	1.5	1.4	2.2
1989–1996	2.0	4.5	4.0	1.8	0.7	2.7	1.6	2.1	2.9	2.0	2.6	1.2	2.3

Notes: Annual data. See text. Parentheses denote average with some countries missing.
Source: Obstfeld and Taylor, 1998.

to use the size of the current account as a percentage of national income. The rationale for this is that the current account is the difference between national savings and domestic investment and corresponds to the net capital flow.

Using this measure of the mean absolute value of the current account expressed as a percentage, capital flows before 1914 were close to 4 per cent of GDP. With foreign lending for war purposes this increased during World War I, peaking at a little over 5 per cent. The troubled inter-war years saw a general fall in capital flows (with some notable exceptions that we deal with elsewhere) and by the 1930s they were down to less than 1.5 per cent of national income. (It has to be borne in mind throughout this discussion that national income was generally higher in the inter-war period than for the late nineteenth century and so this measure does not capture the absolute scale of these flows.) Although, once again, capital flows increased in wartime, they declined in the following period and reached an all-time low in the 1960s, at just above 1 per cent. Thereafter they picked up to around 2–2.5 per cent in the 1980s and 1990s, but this was still well short of where they had been in relative terms in the period before World War I. (For a smaller sample, Eichengreen, 1998, had found broadly similar results.)

There are huge differences between countries, but what stands out is the staggering inflows to the developing economies of the late nineteenth century – Argentina, Australia and Canada. Nothing remotely on that scale shows up again even in recent times, and the scale on which Britain lent (in relation to its output) has never again been equalled – not by the US after World War II nor by Japan in the last two decades.

The other point that might be made about capital flows after World War I is that there were three main bursts. The first was in the first half of the 1920s, the second in the late 1970s and the third in the 1990s. Each was followed by a debt crisis of one kind or another.

This overview is a highly simplified picture that will not surprise anyone with any knowledge of modern economic history. At its simplest it can be expressed as follows. The largely British-inspired liberal order of the nineteenth century saw increasing integration, openness of economies, globalisation. This was under strain from some quarters in the late nineteenth century and certainly put on hold by the outbreak of war in 1914. There was no successful resolution after the war ended in 1918, and international mistrust built on serious disequilibria resulted in depression, fascism and further war. It was only after 1945–50, with widespread acceptance of the problems and a powerful desire to solve them, that the world economy began to grow rapidly again. However, there are still some puzzles. Capital flows did not by any means coincide completely with periods of growth – for example, the 1950s and 1960s were decades of rapid growth but limited capital flows, though clearly capital controls played some part in this. We note too in surveying the international monetary system that the design of the post-war system depended in large part on a particular interpretation of the 1930s experience, specifically that capital flight was a problem and stable exchange rates required controls on capital.

Three explanations have, however, been offered for the main shifts in capital flows.

- The first is that the fixed exchange rate of the gold standard period (1880–1914) generally minimised exchange-rate risk and so promoted flows.

- A second view is related to economic development. Once a basic stage of development is reached, foreign borrowing can take place and gradually high returns fade as development proceeds, so periods of large-scale lending are likely to appear at times when there are large differences in income levels between countries.
- A third view is that there is a twenty-year cycle of boom and bust, triggered by some disturbance that attracts the attention of investors and then goes through a cyclical process. In all three of the surges of lending noted above there were stagnant or falling interest rates in the principal lending countries.

None of these explanations is terribly convincing. The modern world economy has a relatively short history within which to test such observations, especially so given the upheavals there have been and the distinctly different conditions prevailing in a rapidly changing world. Perhaps the first explanation is the least unsatisfactory, but it does raise the question of why exchange-rate stability was not pursued with greater intent by governments after 1918/19. Stabilisation was pursued but without sufficient thought being given to the appropriate rate. In the end, we are left pondering the possibility that it is simply stability in the international system and the greatest freedom from restrictions which explains the flows. There are contrasting views, though. One example can be found in Eatwell (1996), who writes that it is 'no accident that the explosive growth of international capital flows coincided with the 1973 collapse of the Bretton Woods system of fixed exchange rates' (p. 5). This would turn our first and probably best explanation on its head. There are many other things wrong with Eatwell's argument, but it is sufficient at this point to note that it lacks any historical perspective, particularly on the fact that the 1960s was a decade of extremely low capital movement.

The following section abstracts from these difficulties to provide some different perspectives on capital flows and to flesh out the bare bones above. Unless otherwise stated, the flows are both long-term and short-term combined.

Figure 1 summarises the position in 1913 in terms of lenders. It brings out the dominance of the UK and the prominent second position of France. Germany and the US also have substantial shares. Figure 2 summarises the principal destinations in 1913. Exactly half of all long-term capital was in the developed world of Europe, the US and Canada; and Australia and New Zealand could be added to make 55 per cent. Latin America took the biggest share of the balance with over 40 per cent of the less developed world, Africa and Asia having roughly similar shares of 20 per cent. By the end of the inter-war period there is an interesting if unsurprising change (Figure 3). The UK has increased its share to 44 per cent, mostly at the expense of France and Germany, the shares of both of which have shrunk. Not surprisingly, the US has substantially increased its share to 22 per cent. Figure 4 brings out the net capital movements for selected periods – the half-decades from 1881 to 1913. The extreme cases illustrate the usefulness of this approach by showing the UK at the top as the major creditor. France's position in second place also shows clearly; though, interestingly, at early dates Germany was larger. At the other end the US was the largest debtor at several points but moved to being a net creditor at the turn of the century, even if it slipped momentarily from this position in the years 1906–10. Of the twelve major participants shown here, the bulk of the rest are contained within those limits but under the zero line, that is, as recipients. Apart from this, the case of Canada stands out, as it borrowed increasingly heavily in the decade before World War I.

The same exercise is continued in Figure 5 with the period extended to the late 1930s and the 1950s for the US. This shows the falling off in the net movements position of the UK, and the great surge from the US following World War II.

Narrowing the focus still further but taking a very long view, Figure 6 traces the exports of capital from France, Germany and the UK over the period 1833–1993, showing these as a percentage of their respective GDP. (There are large data gaps for the inter-war years.) Figure 7 brings out more clearly the changing position of these three countries in the years 1953–93. For most of the post-war period up to 1970 the three countries are close together, but France was for a larger part a net creditor and Britain a net debtor.

Figure 1   **Total long-term foreign investments by principal creditor countries, 1913**

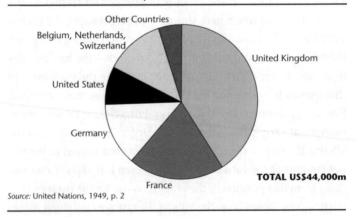

Source: United Nations, 1949, p. 2

Figure 2   **Distribution of foreign long-term investments, 1913**

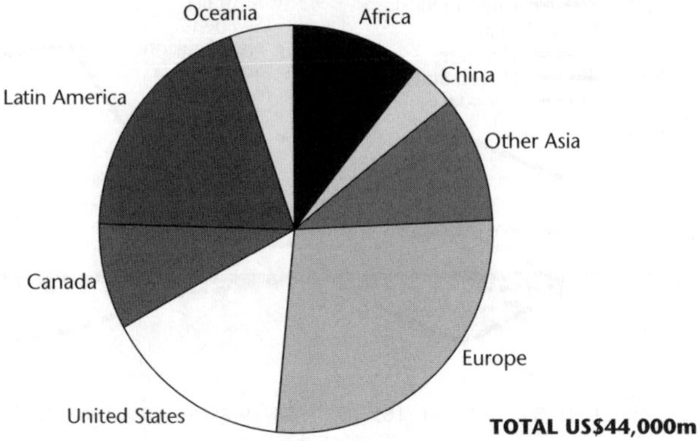

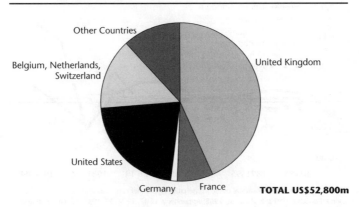

Oceania Africa China Other Asia Latin America Canada United States Europe

TOTAL US$44,000m

Source: Feinstein and Watson, 1995, Table 3.1, p. 97.

Figure 3   **Long-term foreign investment by principal creditor countries, 1938**

Other Countries Belgium, Netherlands, Switzerland United Kingdom United States Germany France

TOTAL US$52,800m

Source: Feinstein and Watson, 1995, Table 3.1, p. 97.

Figure 4   Net capital movements for selected periods pre-1914, US$m

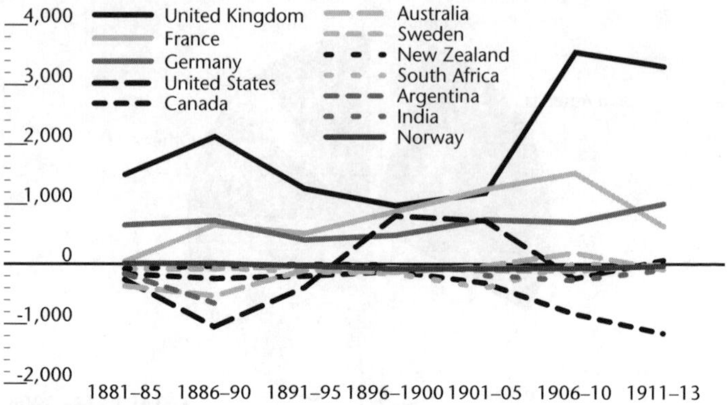

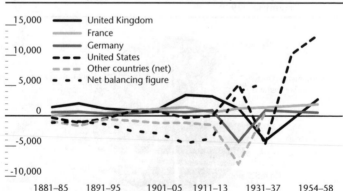

Positive figures denote net capital outflows, negative figures net capital inflows.
Source: Bloomfield, 1968, Appendix 2, p. 47.

Figure 5   Net capital movements for selected periods, US$m

Positive figures denote net capital outflows, negative figures net capital inflows.
Source: Periods to 1913: Bloomfield, 1968, Appendix 2, p. 47; 1924–30, 1931–37: Feinstein and Watson, 1995, Table 3.3, p. 110; 1947–53, 1954–58: United Nations, 1959, Table 2, p. 19.

Figure 6   **A very long-term perspective on exports of capital**
Net capital exports shown as % of GDP/GNP

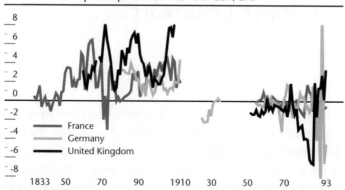

Positive figures denote net exports, negative figures net imports.
Sources: Mitchell, 1998, Tables J1 and J3, except capital exports of Germany (1881–1913) and UK (1860–1913), from Bloomfield, 1968, Appendix 1.

Figure 7   **Post-war exports of long-term capital**
Long-term capital exports expressed as % of GDP

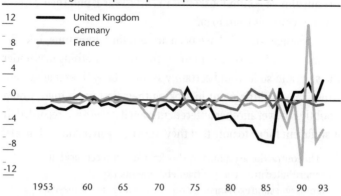

Positive figures denote net capital exports, negative figures net imports.
Source: Mitchell, 1998, Tables J1 and J3.

4 CAPITAL CONTROLS

The terms 'capital controls' and 'exchange controls' are sometimes used as synonyms, and perhaps there is no great harm in this. A quick survey of dictionaries of economics found entries for exchange controls but not capital controls, even in the *New Palgrave*. The term 'exchange controls' is generally thought of as covering both current account transactions and capital account transactions, but it is better thought of as describing the mechanism used to implement capital controls. 'Capital controls' refers specifically to capital account transactions in the balance of external payments. Strictly speaking, there were capital controls in Britain almost continuously from World War I, and then current account controls from 1939.

Exchange controls have been around for a long time. Like Ecclesiastes, the historian is apt to say that there is nothing new under the sun, and so it would certainly seem to be with exchange controls. There is little point in seeking their first use – there would doubtless be yet another antecedent even if it were not recorded. It is sufficient for us to note that they were in use in medieval Europe.

> The contractionary monetary shocks in fifteenth-century Europe resulted in . . . competitive debasements, export embargoes and exchange controls . . . The favourite scapegoats were the financial classes . . . foreign exchange dealers, especially if they happened to be foreigners (Day, 1987: 62).

Day goes on to remark that none of these remedies proved effective. But the quote could just as easily refer to the 1930s, and the danger is that it could be applied again around the turn of the millennium.

The modern use of these controls dates from the 1930s, when they were employed extensively. Like their counterpart, trade controls, they are often imposed in a crisis and then long outlive the crises they were intended to alleviate. Our account has outlined first the evolution of the international monetary system, in effect beginning in the late nineteenth century. That system worked well until it was broken up by World War I. In the period of turmoil that followed, when debt and reparation payments, differential inflation experience and seriously distorted trade all played their part in disrupting the world economy, and more seriously the payments system, it is perhaps not surprising that controls were introduced. Capital flows were distorted as a result of political upheaval, and when exchange controls were widely used in attempts at coping with the various financial and exchange-rate crises of the great depression years (1929–32) the distortions were extended further. The controls that were introduced were often still in place in the 1990s in the developed countries, even if abolition or phasing out was going on from the 1970s.

Although it has been shown that huge capital flows moved without controls, and without problems, before 1914, an important element in the story of the origin of controls was capital movements. World War I, and its unsatisfactory outcome in terms of the resolution of many issues, had created a great deal of political uncertainty in Europe and stimulated a corresponding amount of capital movement. Some of the movement was prompted by fear that the capital would not be able to be moved in anticipated circumstances. From World War I through the 1920s there was capital movement of this kind from all parts of Europe. There was also a 'normal' change in the source and direction of capital flows when, for example, Britain was no longer in the position to lend that she had been in the nineteenth century; and in direction when American investment in Germany began to be returned in the late 1920s as the New York stock exchange boomed.

But the really large movements in capital were provoked by the increasing uncertainty generated at the turn of that decade with the spreading world depression and further political developments, which all raised questions over the exchange rates. When the Nazis emerged as the second-largest party in the Reichstag in 1930, things got worse. In the summer of 1931 the Brüning government introduced exchange controls and a standstill on short-term debt was negotiated. Not surprisingly, capital flight increased. There were fears that the British would do something similar. In September 1931 they did, when they severed the link with gold. As explained below, the Exchange Equalisation Account for managing the exchange rate was introduced the following year. Many other countries followed suit soon after, and of particular importance was the US in 1933. It was at this point that exchange controls began to proliferate.

Another part of the story of the origins of controls lies in the newly designed international monetary system, the principal features of which have already been noted. It is here that we can see the direct link between the 1930s and the design of a new system for the period after World War II. Given what was widely accepted would be Britain's balance of payments position after World War II (limited export potential and continuing high imports of food and raw materials), it was felt that some safeguards would be needed if Britain was to abandon its imperial preferential apparatus (as the US was insisting it do). In order to allow Britain to do this Keynes drafted (in 1941) his proposal for an International Clearing Union – which was the basis of the 'Keynes Plan' for the new international monetary system.

But for Britain, what specifically were the roots of its controls? Regulation of British overseas investment goes back farther than is commonly thought. Although things were essentially free before 1914 in the age of *laissez-faire*, nevertheless there was an exception in that colonial governments got preferential treatment in the London capital market. But it was World War I which brought the first real controls, and these were readily accepted because the government had to have control in order to raise the necessary wartime finance and protect the exchange rate when the link with gold had been cut. In December 1914 controls on overseas lending were introduced, and these were increasingly tightened in the course of the next few years. A Capital Issues Committee was established. After 1919 the Committee was allowed to be more lenient.

After World War I the government had no recognised powers to control foreign lending; influence was exercised by the Treasury, which in turn used the Bank of England to carry out the operations. The Bank organised priorities, with domestic borrowers first, dominion and colonial next, and foreigners last. Much policy in the early 1920s was directed at restoring the gold standard. As the prospect of this became real, so the Bank wanted to reduce the supply of sterling on the foreign exchange market – and thus exert upward pressure on the rate. From November 1924 foreign loans were excluded altogether, and from April 1925 dominion and colonial loans were also excluded. The embargo was removed at the end of 1925 and there followed a period of limited freedom. But the embargo was used again in 1929 when the pound came under pressure; indeed, the embargo came to be seen as an alternative to raising Bank Rate (Atkin, 1970).

Britain adopted different measures for managing the exchange rate in the 1930s. After the abandonment of gold in September 1931 the Exchange Equalisation Account was set up. Initially, it had £175 million (about 4 per cent of GNP, for the sake of some indication of size) and was under the control of the Treasury, which decided what securities it would hold. The ambition was to target a particular exchange rate, and in the process the operators were able to sterilise the effects of capital flows on the domestic money supply. It began operations on 1 July 1932 and set about holding sterling at a value that was consistent with not upsetting other countries and at the same time appearing appropriate for stability. Some new capital controls were introduced in 1931 and 1932, but over the course of the 1930s they were eased rather than tightened.

5 THEORY

The introduction of some basic theory allows for a consideration of the case for (and against) capital flows. International capital flows take place when one country's citizens or government lend to (that is, buy assets of) another country. The former country then has an outflow and the latter an inflow. In terms of the balance of payments, the surplus on the current account is either accumulated as reserves or it flows out as capital, or it is some combination of the two. In the conventional national income framework,

$$Y = C + I + G + (X - M)$$

where Y is income, C is consumption, I is investment, G is government, X is exports and M is imports.

Income that is not consumed is either paid in taxes to government or it is saved, so that an alternative expression of the national income identity is

$$(I - S) + (G - T) + (X - M) = 0$$

where S is savings and T is taxes.

Capital flows thus finance any deficiency between savings and investment (inflow) or excesses of savings over investment (outflow).

If there is a surplus, then a country is capital-abundant and funds flow to countries that are deficient. By allowing the free flow of such capital the world finds that its welfare is raised since a more efficient allocation of resources is achieved, and as a result of greater opportunities being exploited investors get higher risk-adjusted rates of return than would otherwise have been possible. Free capital movements allow for improved portfolio diversification and better risk sharing. Further, in the same way that domestic financial intermediation improves welfare by allowing individuals and firms to choose between present and future consumption, so international capital mobility allows countries to do the same and in the process possibly dampens the amplitude of business cycle fluctuations. Thus with higher rates of return prevailing, savings and investment are encouraged, which is likely to lead to improved economic performance. There is too the added gain for the world that, just as for traded goods, comparative advantage is exploited and countries with a comparative advantage in the production of financial services export such services. Where there is free capital mobility there is competition, and this should develop ever more efficient production. In sum, free capital mobility improves the allocation of resources worldwide.

A brief word can be added about increasing investment. Investment is not something to be pursued for its own sake and neither should it be influenced by government. There is obviously a huge range in the quality of investments that are made. Higher investment ratios need not mean higher rates of economic growth, and it is foolish to try to direct funds into investment. But that is part of the case for free mobility – allowing individuals to seek out the best investments is what is likely to raise growth.

Not everyone accepts this. For example, Eatwell (1996) takes issue and argues that higher investment and growth are the most important test of all: '... growth and sustainable human development are highly correlated' (p. 20). He provides an investment/GDP ratio for a variety of countries for the two periods 1972–81 and 1982–91, and argues that the main finding is that the ratio has fallen as capital liberalisation has become more widespread – most OECD countries had lower investment ratios in the 1980s than in the 1960s, as did nine out of ten countries in Latin America. This, of course, ignores a host of factors, not least that with technological advance developed and less developed countries obtained a huge proportion of their investment needs at a fraction of their former cost. Eatwell argues further that output was lower than it was in the 1960s, which betrays an ignorance of history. In any case, it is now clear that the period 1950–70 was (for good reasons) exceptional in the 150 years of the modern world economy.

But to return to the general case, there are those who reject the case for freedom on the grounds that there is asymmetric information, or some other imperfection in the capital market, which results in inefficiencies. The information problem is said to result in adverse selection or moral hazard or perhaps the 'madness of crowds' – where investors simply do what others do. In the first case it is said that because borrowers have better information than lenders credit quality can be misread, resulting in good firms not getting funds and poor firms getting funds because they borrow in the knowledge that their securities are overvalued.

In the second case moral hazard is said to be a problem because in the borrower/lender relationship the borrower changes behaviour after obtaining the loan. The allegation is that information asymmetry allows him to do this. If this is the case, a proportion of investment projects undertaken will be more risky than they might otherwise be. In the final case it is suggested that investors will be guided not by rational thought but by the behaviour of others. If investors are not well informed they may simply follow others whom they believe to be better informed. To some extent, of course, it is rational to behave in this way. Even if the great bulk of investors are mad it benefits the rational investor to join in a scramble and benefit from the rising price.

There may also be a case against free financial flows if there are domestic distortions. Take, for example, a country that protected its car industry – a capital-intensive industry. If the country were in fact labour-intensive the effect would be to attract capital to a sector where the rate of return was artificially high. This would mean that resources in the world were being allocated less efficiently than they could be. It was this possibility that led Richard Cooper to conclude that free capital mobility should follow trade liberalisation (Cooper, 1998). This is not so much a case against free capital flows as a comment on existing protection and the sequencing of liberalisation.

The main case against free mobility, which depends heavily on asymmetric information, has not gone unchallenged. Imperfections in the capital market are frequently cited as the cause of all kinds of missed opportunities and low investment. The most common imperfection identified is said to be the inability of some to borrow the required funds. As Stigler (1994) pointed out a long time ago, this imperfection is frequently read from high rates of interest that have to be paid by the borrower or earned by the lender. But observing such rates is not a sufficient basis on which to reach a conclusion – 'any more than the fact that some people walk is proof of an imperfection in the automobile market' (p. 242). If there is evidence of a realised rate of return greater than the costs of lending, there is an imperfection; but the argument depends on transaction costs. Most asserted instances of imperfection relate to the failure of capital to move to areas where there are higher returns, but these charges frequently lack the necessary evidence. Small firms are often said to be discriminated against, being dependent on only one source of funds and suffering the price a monopolist can extract. Leaving aside whether or not monopoly is a market imperfection, it is difficult to believe that capital, which is the most mobile of all productive factors, cannot be found. There will be cases of monopoly but probably not as many as is often asserted.

There is incomplete information. But this is not an imperfection if it is not remunerative to acquire complete information. To quote Stigler again:

> ... complete knowledge of prices would require the canvas of all traders. Optimum information would require the canvas of traders only up to the point where the expected marginal return from search equals its marginal costs (p. 245).

The problem is that just because there is a deviation in an outcome from something 'better' the difference is called an imperfection – the nirvana approach, as Demsetz (1969, p. 1) called it. The sensible approach is to take the difference between any actual outcome and an

> alternative real institutional arrangement [which] seems best able to cope with the economic problem; practitioners of this approach may use an ideal norm to provide standards from which divergences are assessed for all practical alternatives of interest and select as efficient that alternative which seems most likely to minimize the divergence.

Where a market solution is said to be wanting it is usually 'corrected' by substituting government or some other non-profit agency. But such a substitute needs to be analysed and the outcome compared to the market solution before its superiority is concluded.

The troublesome problem at the international macroeconomic level is the impossibility of achieving three desirable objectives – sometimes called the impossibility theorem, the inconsistent trinity or the eternal triangle. This was first set out by Mundell (1963). The three desirable objectives are:

* freedom to pursue an independent monetary policy;
* freedom for capital flows; and
* stability in the exchange rate.

Take the last first. If a country decides that it cannot accept an unstable currency, susceptible to portfolio swings, then it pegs its exchange rate. If it is also in favour of free capital mobility then it leaves itself open to speculative attack whenever there are any signs of weakness in a range of economic variables. So it must either fix its exchange rate credibly by, for example, establishing a currency board, or in the extreme joining a monetary union, or it must restrict capital flows. It was the perceived instability of currencies in the inter-war period which led the designers of Bretton Woods to insist on capital controls.

If, on the other hand, governments wish to operate a monetary policy independently of other countries and at the same time allow free capital movement, then the possibility is that the exchange rate is going to move around. Whenever there are signs of an easing of monetary policy (in response to a perceived slowdown in output growth) holders of the currency will sell and the exchange rate will fall. For some countries this may result in quite considerable oscillations in the exchange rate which may at times prove uncomfortable; but it must be weighed against the alternatives.

If free capital movement is insisted upon, or indeed it is simply accepted that restrictions on capital movements can no longer be made to work, then it follows that a country must either fix its exchange rate in a way that is believable (and at the same time relinquish control of monetary policy) or else have a freely floating exchange rate.

A simple application of demand and supply analysis throws light on the effects of controls. Figure 8 brings out the nature of the problem in a highly simplified way, showing the demand for and supply of loanable funds in a domestic market alongside the rest of the world. The price of funds is the real risk-adjusted rate of return. Imagine that at some point, shown here as Q_e, an equilibrium is obtained in the world for a certain quantity of funds supplied and demanded, at a price i_e. Now consider that for a particular country there is a supply and demand for funds shown in the figure as S_B and D_B. According to the way this is drawn there is a shortage of funds (demand exceeds supply by q_1q_2) in this country at the price that obtains in the rest of the world. This hypothetical country, if isolated from the world, would have to pay a higher rate of interest than other countries. If this country is not isolated, and is free to lend and borrow, then there would be a flow of funds to country A – a rightward shift of the supply curve – until finally the higher returns are bid away. Simultaneously, country A's borrowers would be borrowing in the rest of the world and bidding up the cost of funds there. The respective impact of these actions would of course depend on the size of country A.

So, if a country could be isolated from other countries, different

Figure 8   Demand for and supply of loanable funds

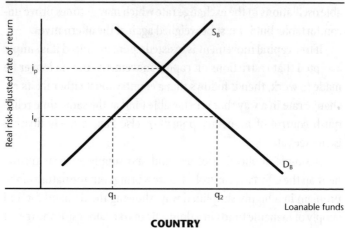

COUNTRY

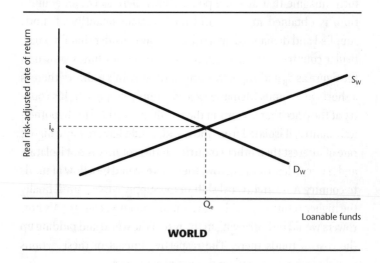

WORLD

Figure 9   **Limiting the import of capital**

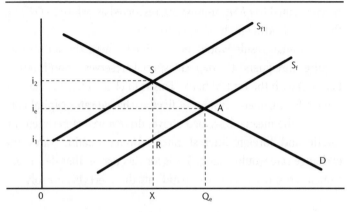

rates of return could be found in the different territories. The principal objective of controls on foreign exchange outflows has been to bring about such isolation to protect official reserves, and on inflows (as noted above) to hold on to domestic monetary autonomy.

There are various ways in which the control of capital flows might be attempted. But there is a clear similarity in impact between quantitative restrictions and taxes or other measures, or at least the similarity can be shown again by means of simple demand and supply analysis (see Phylaktis and Wood, 1984). Figure 9 illustrates how a country importing capital might limit these flows. S_f is the foreign supply of funds and D the domestic demand. An equilibrium is reached at Q_e at a price i_e. Foreigners therefore hold assets equal to OQ_e. The authorities wishing to restrict inflows could place a quantitative limit at a position such as X or alternatively impose a tax on interest that would have the same effect. In the figure a tax equal to $i_1 i_2$ has the effect of moving the supply schedule to the left to S_{f1}. The government collects tax revenue equal to $i_1 RSi_2$, inflows are restricted as before to OX and there is a 'deadweight loss' equal to RAS.

A similar result would be obtained where the authorities require foreigners to deposit special reserves (non-interest-bearing) with the central bank. This is in effect a tax and has the same effect. Under a system of fixed exchange rates capital controls, by the means described above, drive a wedge between domestic and foreign interest rates. (Under floating rates the exchange rate would change.) It is for this reason that deviations from interest parity are used to indicate the effects of controls.

6 THE SPREAD OF CONTROLS

Clearly there is a considerable range of measures which might fall under the heading of exchange control. At one end of the spectrum it could include, at a stretch, the discount policy of the central bank if it were designed to influence the exchange rate. But that is not very helpful in this discussion. What is slightly more problematic, however, just one step along from that, is the operation of an exchange stabilisation account, though these were usually introduced to control bilateral exchange rates. As already noted, such an account was introduced in Britain in the spring of 1932. They also appeared in other countries, notably the US in 1934. However, these are surely more properly regarded as relating to monetary policy rather than commercial policy. They were prompted by the desire to control domestic monetary conditions. The controls that are really of interest in this discussion are the more direct restrictions placed on individuals and firms buying and selling foreign exchange assets. If the desire is to achieve stable exchange rates then the demand for, and supply of, foreign exchange must be kept in balance.

This was usually done by putting foreign exchange business in the hands of one agency such as the central bank. In such a system all foreign exchange earned has to be sold to the bank and all purchases have to be from the bank. Any deviation of the exchange rate from its true value will result in excesses or surpluses with which the bank will have to devise the means of coping. A likely consequence is the emergence of a black market.

In the 1930s different forms of exchange control were introduced, usually as a means of protecting the value of a currency (much as is advocated at present). The proximate cause was generally the prospect or reality of capital flight, the cause of which could depend on a number of other factors and how they were assessed by international investors.

Table 2 (from Aldcroft and Oliver, 1998) brings together some useful data on the abandonment of the gold standard and introduction of exchange controls in the 1930s. This covers most countries in the world, and it shows how a group of countries, mostly with close ties to Britain, abandoned gold at about the same time – September 1931 or soon after. Some others held on until 1933, and the gold bloc countries lasted a bit longer. The abandonment of gold resulted in substantial depreciations, mostly of the order of 40 per cent or more. The table also allows a ready reckoning of how exchange controls coincided with or quickly followed the abandonment of gold, although not every country introduced them. There are one or two cases, of which Austria is an illustration, of countries imposing controls somewhat in anticipation of severing the link with gold, but the great majority of countries introduced controls between the latter part of 1931 and the end of 1933.

However, although the table as it stands gives the appearance of precise dating it does not in any way deal with the hugely different forms of controls that were adopted and extended. Some countries took some mild actions on leaving the gold standard and then relaxed them after just a matter of months. But, for most, the measures taken were to last into World War II and beyond. Part of the problem lay in the great fear of currency depreciation that dated from the chaotic experience that followed World War I. But it was not simply fear of chaos. For debtors, a depreciating currency raised the burden of foreign debt servicing.

Where countries had reasonably robust financial systems – such as Britain, the white dominions (Canada, Australia and New Zealand) and Scandinavia (and it helped to be a creditor) – there tended to be few problems. These countries inclined to the introduction of relatively mild restrictions to stabilise the exchange rate as it floated. Such restrictions typically involved some supervision of applications to buy foreign exchange. Sometimes embargoes were placed on foreign loans. But, in contrast, in most parts of Latin America gold and foreign exchange reserves were low, they were unable to establish stabilisation funds, and as debtor countries they faced capital flight. These countries often set up strict controls which invariably required an array of complicated devices to block the many gaps through which capital would escape. These included such measures as export receipts relating to every sale and the surrender of corresponding foreign exchange. Caught in such traps, exporters would try to leave their earnings outside the country and use such foreign exchange for purchases. But sometimes permits had to be obtained before goods could be shipped, or licences had to be granted. Similar measures extended to goods and financial assets. In Japan in September 1937 a bill was passed requiring the liquidation of all foreign assets held by Japanese subjects, the proceeds to be deposited with the Bank of Japan. The British too had required liquidation of foreign assets in World War I and again in World War II.

On the demand side, similar devices were employed. All kinds of ways around the regulations were tried, which kept the

Table 2 Exchange rates and exchange control in the 1930s

Country	Official suspension of gold standard	Introduction of exchange control	Depreciation or devaluation in relation to gold	Extent of depreciation by early 1935 (%)	Introduction of new gold parity
Albania	—	—	—	—	—
Argentina	17-12-29	13-10-31	11-29	54	—
Australia	17-12-29	—	3-30	52	—
Austria	5-4-33	9-10-31	12-31; 4-34	22	30-4-34*
Belgium	30-3-35	18-3-35	3-35	28	31-3-36*
Bolivia	25-9-31	3-10-31	3-30	59	—
Brazil	—	18-5-31	12-29	59	—
Bulgaria	—	1918	—	—	—
Canada	19-10-31	—	12-31	40	—
Chile	20-4-32	30-7-31	4-32	75	—
China	—	9-9-34	—	50	—
Colombia	25-9-31	25-9-31	1-32	61	—
Costa Rica	—	16-1-32	1-32	44	—
Cuba	21-11-33	2-6-34	4-33	—	22-5-34*
Czechoslovakia	—	2-10-31	2-34; 10-36	16	17-2-34; 9-10-36
Danzig	—	12-6-35	5-35	0	2-5-35
Denmark	29-9-31	18-11-31	9-31	52	—
Ecuador	8-2-32	2-5-32	6-32	73	19-12-35
Egypt	21-9-31	—	9-31	42	—
Estonia	28-6-33	18-11-31	6-33	50	—
Finland	12-10-31	—	10-31	0	—
France	—	—	9-36	0	1-10-36*
Germany	—	13-7-31	—	57	—
Greece	26-4-32	28-9-31	4-32	57	—
Guatemala	—	—	4-33	—	—
Honduras	—	27-3-34	4-33	—	—
Hong Kong	—	9-11-35	—	—	—
Hungary	—	17-7-31	—	—	—
India	26-9-31	—	9-31	40	—
Iran	—	25-2-30	—	57	—
Irish Free State	21-9-31	—	9-31	41	—

Italy	–	2-5-34	3-34; 10-36	4	8-10-36*
Japan	13-12-31	1-7-32	12-31	66	–
Latvia	28-9-36	8-10-31	9-36	–	–
Lithuania	–	1-10-35	–	–	–
Luxembourg	–	18-3-35	3-35	0	1-4-35
Malaya	21-9-31	–	9-31	40	–
Mexico	25-7-31	–	8-31	67	–
Netherlands	27-9-36	–	9-36	0	–
New Zealand	21-9-31	–	4-30	52	–
Nicaragua	13-11-31	13-11-31	1-32	46	–
Norway	28-9-31	–	9-31	46	–
Palestine	21-9-31	–	9-31	–	–
Panama	–	–	4-33	–	–
Paraguay	–	20-8-32	11-29	63	–
Peru	14-5-32	–	5-32	–	–
Philippines	–	–	4-33	–	–
Poland	–	26-4-36	–	42	–
Portugal	31-12-31	21-10-22	10-31	0	–
Romania	–	18-5-32	7-35	52	–
Salvador, El	9-10-31	20-8-33	10-31	40	–
Siam	11-5-32	–	6-32	41	–
South Africa	28-12-32	–	1-33	45	–
Spain	–	18-5-31	1920	44	–
Sweden	29-9-31	–	9-31	0	–
Switzerland	–	–	9-36	–	27-9-36*
Turkey	–	26-2-30	1915	41	–
UK	21-9-31	–	9-31	41	–
USA	20-4-33	6-3-33	4-33	54	31-1-34*
Uruguay	20-12-29	7-9-31	4-29	–	–
USSR	–	–	4-36	19	1-4-36*
Venezuela	–	12-12-36	9-30	23	–
Yugoslavia	–	7-10-31	7-32	–	–

* Provisional parity
– not applicable
Sources: Bank for International Settlements Fifth Annual Report 1934–35 (1935), p. 9; League of Nations (1937), pp. 111–13; from Aldcroft and Oliver, 1998.

authorities busy trying to combat them. The Austrians were believed to censor all registered letters to foreign countries. For some countries banknotes could not be repatriated, and so on.

All of these measures to this point can be described as exchange controls in the broader sense, affecting all foreign exchange whether for current account or capital account transactions. This was typical of the 1930s. But perhaps the restriction placed on gold exports in the US in March 1933 might be considered a capital control more strictly defined.

With the uncertainty that grew at the end of the 1930s Britain introduced 'voluntary' restrictions on 'speculative' forward sales of sterling, and when war was declared on 3 September 1939 formal exchange control was introduced. All other countries that had introduced controls in the 1930s kept them in place through the war and beyond. In Britain in 1947 the Exchange Control Act was passed, but it was largely a re-enactment of wartime regulations. In general, controls stayed firmly in place until the 1950s.

It was then that there began to be some easing, but it was a long and fluctuating process. Resort to controls of one kind or another continued. For example, an interest-equalisation tax was introduced in the US in July 1963, followed by controls on capital outflows at the beginning of 1968 as the US dollar began to feel the pressure that would ultimately force it off the link with gold.

In continental Europe several countries continued with a range of controls. One explanation already noted is that pegged exchange rates needed capital controls. Another is that domestic financial controls were widespread and much of this required capital controls to facilitate their functioning.

The French removed many of their remaining exchange restrictions in January 1967 but they were reintroduced in May 1968, only to be lifted again in September 1968, and reintroduced in November – reactions to the political uncertainty that marked that year. In August 1971, following the last link with gold being abandoned in the US, France restricted capital flows again. The French did not finally remove the last capital controls until 1989, just a matter of months before the EU deadline of 1990. In part, the motivation for removal was the desire to allow Paris to develop as a financial centre.

Italy too had extensive controls, which began in the domestic banking system. Following remarkable economic growth in the decade or so following World War II, Italy slipped into lax monetary and fiscal policies and the concomitant inflation. The lira was weak, and although capital controls were already extensive they were extended further in 1970, and then further again after the lira was more exposed following the breakdown of Bretton Woods.

After World War II Germany had generally pursued as free an economic environment as possible, but in March 1972 Bardepot was introduced in the Federal Republic. This was an exchange control scheme that required German borrowers in foreign markets to deposit part of the proceeds of their borrowing in a non-interest-bearing account at the Bundesbank. Bardepot was thus a disincentive on borrowing abroad by German business and deterred foreign capital flows into West Germany.

With international markets in some turmoil at the beginning of the 1970s following the end of the Bretton Woods period, there was a good deal of toing and froing over the next decade as countries sought to exercise some control over their exchange rate and mitigate the effects of switches in and out of their currencies. But this coincided with the more general mood in favour of liberalisation. The trend was for the removal of restrictions, but there were several points along the way at which governments felt bound to intervene. But the gradual removal of exchange controls in developed countries got under way in the 1970s and in most cases they had gone by the 1990s.

As noted, in March 1972, in the midst of the upheaval in the realignment of currencies, Germany had imposed Bardepot; in June that year the German government, in the face of opposition from the Finance Minister, Schiller, introduced another exchange control measure prohibiting the sale of German bonds to foreigners. In January of the following year, Germany added further exchange control measures. There was some relaxation in January 1974 and then in September Bardepot was lifted entirely. But this was not the end of restrictions: only a few years later other measures were introduced. On 1 January 1978 the Bundesbank imposed a reserve requirement of 100 per cent in increases in the liabilities to non-residents, but terminated these requirements just five months later.

In January 1974 the US announced the termination of controls on capital outflows, though there were in fact some measures still in place which acted as discouragement. These too were to go when in August 1978 the Federal Reserve announced the elimination of the 4 per cent reserve requirement placed on the foreign borrowings of American banks.

Even the Swiss resorted to restriction in 1978 when they prohibited the purchase of Swiss stocks and bonds by foreigners; and then in January 1979 they terminated the ban. They further relaxed controls on capital flows in February 1980. Japan too took measures in March 1978 to discourage capital inflows. In January 1979 it reduced from 100 per cent to 50 per cent the marginal reserves requirements on deposits of non-residents, and then at the end of 1980 lifted many of the controls that were in place.

Thus across the post-World War II period there lay the legacy of the inter-war and war years. There were also the IMF arrangements that allowed the continued use of capital controls. Forces of liberalisation were at work, but there was still frequent resort to controls.

7 BRITISH EXPERIENCE

There had been a number of attempts in Britain at operating on the exchange rate with a view to influencing capital movements, but it was the coming of war in 1939 that saw the introduction of exchange controls. Wartime regulations were introduced under the Emergency Powers (Defence) Act in 1939. In 1947 these were superseded by the Exchange Control Act. That act was the basis for post-war control, although frequent amendment was made. From the outset a key element in applying the controls was 'residency' – people lived either in the sterling area or in the rest of the world, with the Treasury having the power to specify residential status. The sterling area was ring-fenced, and within it there was no difficulty in making payments. Beyond that there was control.

During the war controls of all kinds were extensive and supported by a huge bureaucracy. A principal aim in wartime is to mobilise all the resources possible and direct them to winning the war. There were, therefore, as there had been in World War I, attempts to channel all foreign securities owned by residents through government for sale for desired currencies – generally US dollars – and several restrictions were placed on the sterling assets held by non-residents.

Furthermore, any proceeds from the sale of assets in Britain belonging to non-residents (such as sales of property and disposal of legacies) had to be placed in blocked sterling accounts. They could be used to buy British government securities, and the interest earned on these could be transferred to the holder. Most severe of all was the measure of late 1941 that blocked all bank accounts in Britain whether they were held in the name of British or non-British subjects. All residents had to offer for sale to the Treasury any gold coin and bullion they owned.

In addition to these restrictions, numerous bilateral payments agreements were made with overseas countries to ensure that, as far as possible, trade with them involved only sterling. All of this was perfectly understandable during the war, and to some extent in the period of considerable adjustment immediately after the war. In fact there was some easing of the restrictions after the war as attempts were made to allow sterling to be used more freely.

However, under pressure from the US a premature attempt was made in 1947 to restore substantial convertibility. A provision of the Anglo-US Financial Agreement was that a certain amount of current account convertibility (specified countries) should be restored within a year. However, the rush into dollars that began to take place resulted in the right to make sterling payments to the dollar area being withdrawn. Furthermore, by a variety of means unauthorised transactions were being made which meant a further loss of dollars from the sterling area.

Restrictions continued across the board. Travel allowances were introduced, then abandoned, reintroduced, raised and lowered. Complicated payments arrangements were made, for example, for oil and films. But from the early 1950s, and in some ways helped by the establishment of the European Payments Union, a gradual process began that would lead to convertibility. On the one hand, an ambition of the time was to liberalise trade, and this required payments liberalisation. Against that a system of pegged (not fixed) exchange rates required some form of capital control. Bit by bit, by a variety of means, convertibility was approached. To a considerable extent it was achieved *de facto* in the mid-1950s, but it was on 27 December 1958, when *non-residents* could freely convert sterling, that convertibility was said to have been achieved.

No sooner was this small landmark reached than in 1961 economic difficulties emerged and the gradual dismantling of controls came to an end, and was in some ways reversed. For example, in mid-1961 restrictions were placed on direct investment outside the sterling area. In 1965, under the recently elected Labour government, these restrictions were tightened, and in May 1966 tightened further. Also in 1965 the right of British residents to sell the proceeds of certain items in the investment currency market and receive the sterling premium was removed, and 25 per cent of any sale of foreign securities had to be sold in the official exchange market. These measures were designed particularly to improve the reserves. There were continuing problems with sterling from 1964 onward, though there was some resolution in the devaluation of November 1967. Then steps were taken in 1968 to disengage from the sterling area as necessary for exchange liberalisation. This was going to take some time to effect, and before it was completed came the exchange turbulence of the 1970s. There followed more tightening of exchange controls, which continued in place until 1979.

Leaving aside the issue of sterling's continuing difficulties, it is worth considering why controls remained for such a long time in the UK. Many people reached middle age without having known any other regime. There are several possible reasons, which we consider briefly here. One widespread perception was that the

British economy was essentially weak and vulnerable and needed all the protection it could justify in a world of increasing liberalisation. The case for this is not very strong, and it is no stronger when attention is moved to the balance of payments. The idea that the balance of payments is weak or in constant crisis is a view running through much of the literature on British post-war economic history, and for the most part it does not make sense. By definition the balance of payments balances. But even accepting the implicit story that Britain needed to borrow 'too much' to make it balance, the case is still not strong.

There was undoubtedly a period after World War II when exchange rates were fixed at inappropriate parities and when there was a dollar shortage. Britain's capital account had been weakened by the loss of overseas assets and the acquisition of wartime debts. It took until the late 1950s to pay off excess sterling balances. This was a period when the US had vast productive power and when the other industrial countries were making their way back to full capacity and production. Many materials and goods were available only in the US, and there was a huge demand for them. At the exchange rates chosen there were insufficient dollars to allow their purchase. Clearly in these conditions balance-of-payments problems could arise. But that story cannot really be carried very much beyond the first decade after the war.

The real sources of difficulties in external accounts are the exchange rate and domestic policy. Under a fixed or pegged exchange rate system fiscal policy is the principal culprit, and under a floating rate monetary policy. If either of these is lax, fears of over-borrowing or of inflation and ultimate depreciation lead to pressure on the currency. As D.H. Robertson, writing in the 1950s, put it,

> what are politely called 'balance of payment difficulties' do
> not necessarily drop like a murrain from heaven, but that
> any nation which gives its mind to it can create them for
> itself in half an hour with the aid of the printing press and a
> strong trade union movement (1954: 56).

In other words, the fault lay with the monetary and fiscal authorities and the solution was to attend to domestic economic policy. The pursuit of prudent finance would persuade observers that prices would be stable and the exchange rate robust. Market observers have been watching such variables for a very long time – certainly since the nineteenth century.

A second and related point is one that can be seen in better perspective from the beginning of a new century – that it was the dead hand of the state that lay across policy-making. During World War I all manner of controls were adopted bit by bit as governments sought to direct affairs to winning the war. In the hugely distorted years following World War I there was a desire to return to the patterns of the nineteenth century. But there were to be too many problems that needed attention, and there was an accompanying belief developing that governments could take action to alleviate the problems. This was all given a fillip during the great depression years (1929–32 and beyond for some), when free trade was abandoned and it became clear that there was a decided movement towards the managed economy. World War II allowed a considerable increase in controls of all kinds, and in the aftermath of war there seemed to be a need to persist with controls. Additionally, Britain elected a distinctly socialist government in 1945, one which implemented extensive measures of control through nationalisation of industry and other means.

This was the climate that prevailed for at least the next

twenty years, a climate in which it was implicitly assumed that the state knew best, where endless evidence of market failure and the need for regulation were found. All manner of official statements carry this tone without the slightest hint of reservation or doubt. So, for example, in relation to exchange controls the Bank of England *Quarterly Bulletin* stated: 'By 1956 practically no outward investment that was controlled from the United Kingdom and *would show a reasonable economic advantage to this country* was refused' (Bank of England, 1967: 256; italics added), reflecting the deeply rooted belief that wise bureaucrats knew better than self-interested investors.

There was also the legacy of the 1930s. A common interpretation of that decade was that capital flight of a destabilising kind took place, and it was clear that capital controls were needed to prevent such flight. This view, as we have seen, lay behind Keynes's scheme for an international clearing union, based on the idea that pegged exchange rates would need capital controls to allow them to work. The Bretton Woods arrangements were essentially such a system. It has long been realised that it was a misreading of the inter-war years which led to this. The core of the problem was exchange rates and weak domestic policy. Following the hyperinflation of the early 1920s the markets looked for signs of lax policy. Moreover, the political upheavals led to fears of either lax policy or restrictions on capital flows, thus provoking capital flight.

A final explanation for the persistence of exchange controls long after they served any useful purpose, if ever they did, was the old chestnut: the sluggishness of the City of London (lack of energy, lack of interest, incompetence or whatever). This, though, should surely be put aside. Too much evidence has accumulated to show that, although the City was not without faults, it continued to adapt and must be seen as no worse than any other such centre. Fault can always be found, but the answer to our question must lie elsewhere.

There is always the possibility that controls simply did not work. If that were the case, there would be nothing to answer. They were simply an irrelevance. To some extent this was the case, because a good proportion of external sterling transactions escaped control by virtue of the laxity of controls in 'outer-sterling area' countries in respect of non-sterling countries. As they were easily evaded, there was nothing to get excited about. There were certainly people who held such views in the early 1960s. David Kynaston has quoted at length from an internal Bank of England memo from Sir Maurice Parsons (Executive Director at the time and later a Deputy Governor) to the Governor, Lord Cromer, in April 1963: 'The fact is that there is now a wide measure of agreement between the Bank and the Treasury regarding the ineffectiveness and irrelevance of exchange controls as regards current problems' (paper presented to City University, October 1999, p. 3).

However, if it were generally true that controls did not work there would be other puzzling questions to answer. Why was there so much rejoicing when abolition came? And why were there substantial portfolio shifts in the period immediately after abolition? It is possible there were short periods within which controls did not work. Some evidence for this might be found in the behaviour of the investment premium. However, this tended to rise and oscillate more towards the end of the period of exchange controls, suggesting that policy was more effective then than earlier. One factor that would have reduced the effectiveness of controls, and done so increasingly, was the establishment and growth of the eurocurrency markets. These markets, based in London, meant that capital was available from overseas.

Nevertheless, the reintroduction of some analytical framework can be helpful. British citizens who wished to acquire foreign assets had to buy them from the investment currency pool, which was a pool of privately owned foreign assets. Residents could buy and sell this foreign currency at negotiated rates of exchange. For most of the period these transactions took place at a premium over the official exchange rate, known as the investment currency premium.

Figure 10 captures in a highly simplified fashion the market for foreign currency. There is a demand for foreign currency and a supply, and left alone these will produce an exchange rate. Assume for the sake of argument that this rate is P_1 and is the central parity agreed with the IMF, the rate of $2.80 following the devaluation of 1949. With controls in place the part of foreign exchange available for foreign investment can be shown as OQ_2. Therefore the premium that had to be paid was P_1P_2. Of course, the demand schedule could move around – in and out, and even change its slope over time. The investment currency pool was also able to grow or shrink according to the sale or purchase of certain assets. Thus the investment currency premium, or what was generally called the 'dollar premium', was able to fluctuate and did so quite widely, as is shown in Figure 11. (This shows the effective premium. The nominal premium was based on the last official rate whereas the effective premium reflected adjustment for the current market rate.)

The effective premium was generally quite low and gently fluctuating throughout the 1950s and early 1960s. Thereafter it rose and fluctuated steeply. The nominal premium was as high as 100 per cent on occasions. All that volatility represents uncertainty and must be counted as an added cost. All of this suggests

Figure 10 **The market for foreign currency**

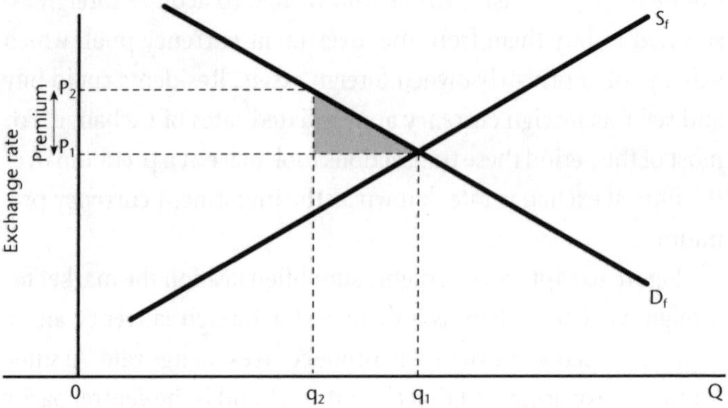

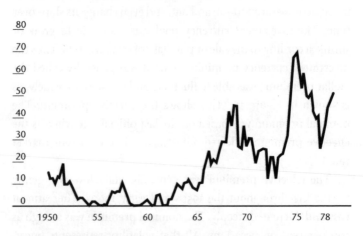

Figure 11 **Effective investment currency premium, 1950–78**
End of quarter figures %

Sources: Bank of England *Statistical Abstracts* Vols 1 and 2; Bank of England *Quarterly Bulletin.*

that controls did work, though the next question is, how important was the pool? The liquid element in the pool was sometimes as low as £50 million at a time when the whole pool was £6,000 million. So it may be that, although there is the appearance of a hugely inflated price being charged, it may have applied to a small proportion of the investing population (Bank of England, 1976).

Drawing the demand and supply curves points to the possible costs and benefits of losers and gainers. It does depend on the respective elasticities of these curves, but the shaded triangle in Figure 10 (the welfare triangle) represents the 'deadweight loss' – that is, the bureaucratic burden, armies of officials, and so on. Miller and Wood (1979) estimated that 4,650 people were employed in the administration of controls at a cost of £50 million, and this is certainly part of the deadweight loss.

What can be said about the impact and importance of the abolition of exchange controls? There are several possible channels through which the impact might work. These range over the psychological, the international economic and the domestic macroeconomic; but it is difficult to be precise about any of them. Some recent discussion has given abolition of controls a major role in the ensuing change. For example, Michie says, 'there can be no doubt that the abolition of exchange controls in October 1979 was fundamental as it created the conditions that encouraged ... a transformation' (1999: 544). Change became inevitable as competition in international capital markets was allowed to develop. This was not necessarily foreseen by the government of the day, as Michie notes:

> ... there is nothing to suggest that the Conservative
> government was even remotely aware that the ending of

> exchange controls had implications for the Stock Exchange,
> let alone ones that would undermine the whole way it had
> developed over the last thirty years (1999: 545).

One of the most difficult effects of abolition to comment on is the psychological significance of the decision, which was taken just a matter of months after the new Conservative government took office in 1979, but it was clearly of some importance. There were several indications that the new government would be more radical than its Conservative predecessors. And there was a great deal of rejoicing, particularly among the public and small investors, when abolition came. They immediately bought foreign property which had previously been denied them, and generally felt better for the freedom they had been given. How big this shift in investment was is something to which we return.

What was the macroeconomic impact? This is an impossible question to answer. There were simply too many other factors coincident with abolition to allow any disentangling of the respective effects. For example, at the same time the US effected a policy regime change when the Federal Reserve tightened money sharply, which sent interest rates rising and had a large effect on exchange rates and expectations more generally around the world. There was too the second oil price hike of the late 1970s, which was continuing to have its effects. At this point the UK had become an oil exporter and the impact of oil price rises on the economy was dramatically different from that on Britain's industrial competitors.

Perhaps of more significance than these external changes was the fact that the Thatcher government was embarking on a range of macroeconomic policies which were having important effects on the economy. There was the increased attention given to monetary policy and the announcement of a clear intention to monitor and control money supply. (Whether it was monitored and controlled does not matter greatly for the present argument so long as it affected expectations in the financial markets at the time. Pepper and Oliver have argued that this is precisely what the ambition of the Treasury was.) Also, public expenditure was to be more tightly controlled and there was considerable confidence that the intentions would be realised. Whatever the reasons, over the next fifteen months the pound soared and then began to fall for several years.

On the microeconomic front there were, as might have been expected, mixed effects. The most important was what happened to the City of London. There were, of course, casualties, such as the 700 people who immediately lost their jobs at the Bank of England, but the consensus is that City business, again as might have been expected, improved. How much is still hard to say, but the improvement probably accelerated over the following decade. This raises the question once more as to why there was not more pressure from the City to have the controls removed. There is agreement too that abolition stimulated the international investment management business, which prospered hugely in London.

Something else to bear in mind is that the abolition took place in a world in which liberalisation of international trade and payments was taking place. There was international pressure for removal of controls, and Britain was one of the few industrial countries to persist with them for so long. So there was probably much less surprise at the action in 1979 than, say, at some comparable kind of action, such as the Labour government's granting of independence to the Bank of England in May 1997. Nevertheless, it is interesting to consider the extent of the portfolio shift that took place. This we do below in the context of some Labour Party proposals of the time.

The abolition of controls in October 1979 did not guarantee that Britain would stay free of such controls. At the beginning of the 1980s many in the Labour Party were in favour of reintroducing exchange controls when they returned to power, which at that time many believed would be at the next election in 1983. That did not happen, but in the mid-1980s the Labour Party was still reiterating this intention. A pamphlet titled *Investing in Britain* set out proposals on how to realise it. A long-running complaint about the British economy (one that dates back in its modern form to the late nineteenth century) is that money flows abroad, largely at the instigation of City institutions, and that this deprives British industry of much-needed investment funds.

Specifically, the complaint is that economic growth (and hence employment) is a function of investment and the latter was too low. That it was too low was demonstrated by a cross-section comparison of international investment ratios. According to this the Japanese invested approximately 32 per cent of their GDP while the British invested around 12 per cent. The blame for the investment ratio being too low fell on the City, which did not provide proper channels for domestic or foreign savings. The problem was said to have reached a new dimension:

> ... since the removal of exchange controls (1979)
> institutions have invested far too large a proportion of their
> funds abroad ... The City's efforts have not therefore
> concentrated on the needs of the domestic economy (p. 12).

With the problem thus identified, the cure for the British disease was seen to lie in the prevention of capital outflows, the repatriation of overseas assets and the establishment of a National Investment Bank (NIB) to direct these assets into British industry at subsidised rates. The plan was to penalise institutions that lent abroad. The attention was on pooled investment schemes (pension funds and unit trusts in the main), with the position on individuals less clear. The proposed scheme required that the overseas content of institutions' portfolios should not exceed a given percentage (hinted to be about 5 per cent). So imagine that a pension fund picked a winner in some foreign equity and at that point held the full quota of its portfolio in such assets. If the equity then soared in value relative to domestic equities without the fund doing anything, it would still have been compelled to sell some of this exciting stock in order to hold to the tolerable proportion in its portfolio. 'Freedom of choice will remain,' said the document, but anyone not complying with the directive would be taxed. And 'freedom of choice' would be extended to the funds being compelled to place a certain proportion of their portfolios in the loan stock of the NIB.

The result of this scheme would 'in all probability be a substantial repatriation of capital ... and a sharply diminished outflow in the future'. The Labour Party envisaged that at least £20 billion would be repatriated. (As we shall see shortly, that would be more than all the new overseas investment between 1980 and 1984.) If all the funds and trusts disobeyed they would have paid an estimated £4 billion in taxes. But for those who complied, the amount repatriated would be invested in the loan stock of the NIB. That stock would carry a 'market' rate of interest. The NIB would then pass the money on to worthy borrowers at subsidised rates of interest. The anticipation was that high on the list among the borrowers would be the newly established enterprise boards. In the light of the investigations of the Greater London Enterprise Board (GLEB) in the 1980s, if that did not fill the investor with a deep sense of foreboding nothing would.

The focus was on overseas *portfolio* investment. *Direct* investment was a separate issue and there was no intention, at least initially, of compelling British companies to sell factories abroad and build in Britain instead. The evidence on this complicated issue regarding the impact of direct investment overseas is that it is certainly not a substitute for domestic investment, and indeed that the overall and continuing effect has been positive (Reddaway, 1968). The second point worth making is that there was some confusion in the two strands in the proposals. One suggestion was to repatriate 'excessive' flows abroad. The other was to channel these through the NIB. (This would therefore have converted overseas portfolio investment into direct domestic investment.) This latter means of encouraging investment does not have a convincing history – not even the German experience of the Kreditanstalt der Wiederaufbau, originally set up to channel Marshall aid funds but later used to provide loans to small and medium-sized firms (Edwards and Fischer, 1994) – and must be regarded as a political gesture. The Japanese were at this stage on the point of abandoning their version of the NIB. It is the first part of the proposals which is of chief concern, the forced repatriation of overseas assets.

First of all, for the sake of argument accept that the diagnosis of the problem was correct – too much money was flowing abroad and a certain amount should have been redirected to the domestic economy. What then would be the scale of the problem? According to the argument, implicitly there was some equilibrium, or at least a tolerable level of overseas investment, around 1979, for what was wanted was a repatriation roughly equal to the sum of the flow of funds abroad that had taken place since that date.

After the abolition of exchange controls in October 1979 there was a flow of funds abroad. At the end of 1979 the stock of net

Table 3 **Change in net external assets**

	£bn	% GDP
1980	3.5	1.5
1981	7.0	2.8
1982	5.0	1.8
1983	2.5	0.8
1984	0	0

Source: Treasury Economic Progress Report, February 1985.

external assets was approximately £12.56 billion. By the end of 1984 that stock had risen in value to £70 billion. However, the great bulk of this increase arose from the changing value of the assets rather than new investment – much of the increase was attributable to the rise in the dollar and hence the increased value of all assets when translated into sterling. Of the overall increase of £57.5 billion, £42 billion was attributable to changing values of the assets and the balance to new investment. (To a certain extent the increase in value of the assets confirms the wise selection.) The new investment was roughly as shown in Table 3.

The figures on new portfolio investment for the non-bank private sector are as shown in Table 4, which shows a slightly higher figure than the change in net assets – a total of £21.9 billion. This gross figure is useful as an indicator of the total extent of funds going into foreign securities. For some purposes we would want to deduct the inward flow of funds to British securities. This would reduce the figure of £21.9 billion to £16 billion. It is perfectly possible that, without any intervention, at a future point the inflow could exceed the outflow.

Working on the basis that the analysis of the problem was correct, these figures show that the British economy was 'deprived' of investment funds to the tune of about 1.5 per cent of GDP each

Table 4 **Flows and stocks of portfolio investment**

	Flows (£bn)	Stocks (£bn)	% change in stocks
1980	4.0	16.8	47.5
1981	4.9	22.2	32.1
1982	5.2	33.8	52.3
1983	4.8	49.6	47.0
1984	3.0	63.0	26.8
Total	21.9		

Source: Calculated from MQ5 *Business Monitor* 1985.

year. The fact that the Japanese had an investment ratio of 32 per cent and the Germans 25 per cent, while Britain's was only 12 per cent, would suggest that even if *all* of these repatriated funds had been compulsorily channelled into new real investment in Britain, they would have raised the investment ratio to 13.5 per cent. This would not go very far towards explaining differential growth rates between Britain and most other countries. Therefore such a change was unlikely to improve, let alone correct, British growth and alleviate unemployment.

This analysis of what happened to capital flows from Britain following the abolition of controls suggests that there was the expected portfolio shift, and that thereafter the flow stabilised. It also suggests that there is no evidence that the City was an obstructive agent, nor that any redirection of the flows that took place would have resulted in any improvement in economic performance.

8 THE RETURN OF CONTROLS

In spite of the lessons of historical experience there are no particular reasons why exchange controls should be seen as a thing of the past, any more than that barriers to trade and services should be seen as such. Protectionism in trade is unlikely ever to go away so long as there are beneficiaries in a position to influence events. And protection has never gone away. Although most economists regard free trade as the preferred policy stance, there are always pressure groups that argue for protection in certain circumstances, and there are capitulating governments who grant it. The problem is that protectionist policies, once adopted, have proved very difficult to remove. Although there has been a concerted effort over a long period for increased trade liberalisation, in the world at large and via international institutions, still the threat bubbles away just below the surface.

So it is with controls on capital. In the 1980s and 1990s the argument appeared again. The story was that there had been huge and destabilising flows of short-term capital and that some restrictions needed to be imposed to dampen them and their effects. This ignores the true cause of the problem, with which we deal briefly in this section; namely, poorly conceived banking systems with defective incentive structures, operating in countries with pegged exchange rates and sometimes defective macro policy.

No sooner had the pegged exchange-rate system of Bretton

Woods – a system that had been supported by capital controls, which indeed was in important respects possible only with such controls – broken down at the beginning of the 1970s than suggestions were being made for other kinds of controls on capital flows. The most notable of these proposals was that of James Tobin, who proposed a 'global tax on foreign exchange transactions' in a lecture he gave in 1972. This was published in 1974. Then a more explicit statement was made in 1978. What lay behind this was a desire to discourage speculation – inevitably resulting in a lower degree of international capital mobility. Tobin (1978) wrote, 'we need to throw some sand in the well-greased wheels' of international financial markets by imposing a tax on all foreign exchange transactions. His ambition was to diminish transactions without affecting 'genuine' investment. He argued that a 0.2 per cent tax on each foreign exchange transaction would amount to a 48 per cent tax on every business day trading (that is, 0.2 × 240 days = 48 per cent) but reckoned that this would have a minimal effect on long-term investment. According to some, however, the proposal to discourage speculative activity would actually have increased overshooting instead of reducing it. More damaging, and making the proposal entirely infeasible, was that the taxes would have to be implemented in all countries simultaneously.

One of the most distinguished international economists, Jagdish Bhagwati, has long been an ardent advocate of free trade and a savage critic of protectionist barriers of any kind. Indeed, when the 'new international economics' emerged, with some of its adherents demonstrating that under certain circumstances trade protection could be beneficial, Bhagwati dismissed them. But when it comes to trade in capital he has argued (Bhagwati, 1978) that things are different. He suggests that trade in goods is not subject to herd behaviour or panics or associated features in the way that capital is, so capital flows can be damaging and some controls are desirable. The case does not have much strength and indeed Obstfeld and Rogoff (1996) demonstrated that the gains from trade extended to trade in financial instruments and that Bhagwati's concerns were misplaced.

Many others have joined in, so there is now a list of eminent economists who are prepared to advocate exchange controls, and a number of practitioners such as George Soros who would lend support to such advocacy.

One country that adopted this advice was Chile, which is otherwise a follower of free market principles, and so was among the most recent and notable countries to implement controls on capital inflows in 1978–82 and again when they were reintroduced in 1991. The background to Chile's recent experience lies in a fragile banking system. The former finance minister of Chile, Sergio de la Cuadra, outlined with great candour what went wrong (de la Cuadra and Valdes, 1992). In the 1980s there were perverse incentives such that banks were more willing to take on credit risk derived from exchange-rate and interest-rate risk. From the early 1980s there was a *de facto* government guarantee to cover exchange-rate risk. Not surprisingly, debts to banks increased hugely. The devaluation of June 1982 quickly inflicted losses on the holders of dollar-denominated debts. The central bank allowed banks to defer losses over several years. Loans to non-bank firms that had connections with banks through conglomerates were plentiful as a result of the government guarantee. This was the background, against which it was not surprising to find foreign investors keen to participate. Thus it was that, with huge dangers looming, the Chileans introduced controls in 1991. The restrictions can be summarised as follows. Firms borrowing foreign currency were required to deposit a 20 per cent reserve in a non-interest-bearing account at the central bank. It had to remain there for one year. That requirement was raised to 30 per cent in May 1992, and was then subsequently reduced to 10 per cent in June and removed in September 1998. There were no restrictions on the repatriation of profits on any foreign direct investment. However, the initial investment had to remain in the country for a minimum of twelve months. The basic objective of the requirements was to dampen short-term flows without affecting long-term flows.

How effective were controls in Chile? Before summarising some of the findings, it is interesting to note that it is difficult to discover what the penalties were for violation of the rules. Presumably there were substantial fines and even tougher penalties, but given the great difficulties of policing and enforcement the other thing that seems to be missing from the discussion is what the costs of the controls were.

Trying to establish the effectiveness of the controls is of course far from easy, but we can start at the simple end of the spectrum with an examination of the pattern of capital flows and external debt in the course of the 1990s. According to the IMF, Chile's short-term debt was US$3,462 million in 1988, having increased from US$3,078 million in 1977, but it had risen and fallen in between times. It had peaked at US$6,497 million in 1994. The Bank for International Settlements (BIS) data showed a similar change in the composition of the debt. Sebastian Edwards (1999b) gives a quite different picture. His Table 7 shows gross capital inflows from 1988 to 1996. Short-term loans in 1988 of US$916,654 million peaked in 1990 at US$1,683,149 million and then fell away to a trivial US$67,254 million in 1996. As a percentage of total inflows short-term loans were over 96 per cent in 1988, but they were to fall in every single year after that, dropping hugely in 1991 and 1992 to 72.7 and 28.9 per cent respectively and finishing in 1996 at only 3.2 per cent. Unfortunately, there is insufficient information in the tables to allow a proper consideration of this, but on the face of it there would seem to be a strong case for saying that controls on short-term inflows were effective. However, it is of note – as Edwards points out – that although net short-term private inflows in the balance of payments fell in 1991 after the imposition of controls, net errors and omissions and misinvoicing rose that year, perhaps a reflection of attempts by the private sector to circumvent the restrictions.

However, that is a casual starting point. There have been many more serious attempts to assess the impact, including that by Edwards himself. The usual starting point is to consider the difference between domestic and offshore interest rates, or to test for covered interest parity. Chile did not have an offshore rate, making such assessments difficult. Edwards has made perhaps the most ambitious objective assessment in attempting to measure three different kinds of indicators of effectiveness (Edwards, 1999b).

He first looked at evidence that composition had been affected. Second, he asked whether the dynamic response of the real exchange rate had been affected. Third, he considered the effect on domestic interest rates *vis-à-vis* international rates. For the first he drew on the table cited above. On the second he found that the impact of restrictions on the real exchange rate was very limited and short lived. On the third he found that there was no significant effect on interest rate behaviour and so 'contrary to the authorities' goals, capital controls did not give them greater control over monetary policy' (Edwards, 1999b: 27). Edwards showed that Chile's controls were subject to considerable evasion and concluded more generally:

> Controls on capital inflows are clearly insufficient to eliminate financial instability ... [In Chile] the main cause behind the crisis was a poorly regulated banking sector, which used international loans to speculate in real estate and extended large volumes of credit to the owners of the banks (1999b: 78).

Some controls were also introduced in the Far East in the turmoil of the late 1990s. It is important to remember what the main sources of the capital flows were in that region, and the prevailing problems in the banking systems. The two important sources of capital for Thailand, Indonesia, Korea and Malaysia were Japan and Hong Kong. In the ten years up to 1997, these four countries were the principal recipients of Japanese investment. For several years before 1997 (the planned date for the transfer of the colony of Hong Kong to China), funds not unnaturally flowed out of Hong Kong to many destinations, but much of it into these four relatively close neighbours. There were forces at work which had led to the drying up, and in some cases the reversal, of the flows of these respective sources. In the case of Hong Kong, it was the belief that began to take hold that China would after all allow the kind of independence it had indicated. This kind of event will happen and need not have brought great problems, but it was compounded by the cessation of Japanese investment, a much more serious issue. The problems in Japanese banking have been talked about for some time – in essence their holding of long-term equity of the firms to which they were lending – and have been exacerbated by the government's role. The government is itself a competing financial intermediary through its monopoly postal system, a system that holds government debt as its principal asset. The banking system has had to compete for limited Japanese deposits and has used the leveraging mechanism to do this, safeguarded in large part by the implicit guarantee given by government. The banking system became overextended and government began cutting off finance to it. The banks then called in their loans to subsidiaries and correspondent banks around Asia. These actions brought out more clearly the problems that obtained in the banking systems of these countries – some of them consciously modelled on the Japanese.

Malaysia had experienced considerable economic growth, like the other 'tiger' economies in the 1980s. But then things turned sour. In 1993/94 large capital inflows were attracted for the reasons we have suggested, and then, as crisis loomed, Malaysia imposed controls on inflows. Banks were subjected to a ceiling on 'non-trade or non-investment' related external liabilities, and residents were prohibited from selling short-term monetary instruments to foreigners. Commercial banks had to deposit the ringgit funds of foreign banking institutions with Bank Nejara in non-interest-bearing accounts. The more notable controls were those on outflows, which date from September 1998. The important measures announced were liquidation of offshore accounts by residents and non-residents, a one-year holding period requirement before the sale of Malaysian securities, and a ban on the provision of credit facilities to non-residents.

The principal objective was to allow some independence in monetary policy, and after the controls were imposed interest rates were lowered without apparently putting pressure on the exchange rate. It is too soon for any serious analysis of the effects of these controls to be carried out.

9 THE REAL PROBLEM AND ITS SOLUTIONS

In the recent turmoil in the world economy, with financial crises of one kind or another appearing around the globe, capital flows have been identified as the culprit. The most frequent expression of the problem is that capital moves too unpredictably and too quickly. Somehow this volatility must be dampened, so capital controls have been touted as the solution. This looks very much like a repeat of the misreading of the inter-war years. The real problems have in fact been faulty exchange rates, weak financial systems, inept central bank action and misguided interference by international institutions.

What has been becoming clear for some time, and has been gaining ever more adherents, is that the world of pegged exchange rates is over. The fixed exchange-rate regime that was the gold standard was one in which internal balance was essentially sacrificed to external balance. The parity was held, and whatever pain there might have been was referred elsewhere. The attempt at pegged rates has failed, since these have lacked full credibility and markets will not tolerate poor fiscal or monetary behaviour. Any such behaviour will be dealt with by a withdrawal from that particular currency.

There has long been an argument in favour of floating exchange rates. Although in some senses the world economy lived for generations with a fixed-rate system based on metals, when that broke down at the time of World War I the seeds were sown for floating rates or else completely different arrangements. As early as 1953, Milton Friedman argued against fixed but adjustable rates:

> Because the exchange rate is changed infrequently and only to meet substantial difficulties, a change tends to come well after the onset of the difficulty, to be postponed as long as possible, and to be made only after substantial pressure on the exchange rate has been accumulated. In consequence, there is seldom any doubt about the direction in which an exchange rate will be changed, if it is changed. In the interim between the suspicion of a possible change in the rate and its actual change, there is every incentive to sell the country's currency if a devaluation is expected ... or to buy it if an appreciation is expected (Friedman, 1953: 169).

The case has been argued more persistently in recent years until an overwhelming consensus has emerged. The exceptions might be where countries seek less volatility in the exchanges and prefer a currency or monetary union; in the process they give up control of their monetary policy. Some small countries with a poor history of inflation have opted for establishing a currency board. If they are small enough either not to matter greatly in international finance or, more likely, to be sufficiently transparent and completely credible in their actions, they could succeed. But otherwise the case for floating rates looks overwhelming. With floating rates currency crises are unlikely, as the rate is constantly responding to all manner of news items.

That said, there will nevertheless continue to be financial crises, which have been around for as long as there have been financial markets. But at least there should be less talk of contagion with a floating-rate system established. Under the gold standard in the late nineteenth century it was quite clear that a financial crisis in one country could be (indeed was likely to be) transmitted through the system (Bordo, 1986). The case for floating rates is that they cushion against such shocks and allow independence in monetary policy. But that is why it is important to distinguish between a financial crisis and a currency crisis, and to be clear that they need not go together.

There are many views of financial crises and as many definitions, ranging from a narrow focus on money to a very loose consideration of the price of almost any asset. It seems much more useful to concentrate on the narrow view. This would argue that a financial crisis is something which threatens the money stock – some set of events and circumstances which is in imminent danger of bringing about a sharp decline in the money stock. It is the peril of such an outcome that makes it the sensible focus. A decline in the money stock in the face of wage and price stickiness has a deleterious impact on real output.

It is for the same reason that the collapse of a non-bank financial institution does not bring (or should not bring) the same concerns. The failure of a large investment bank, for instance, or of a large insurance company, will undoubtedly be unpleasant for the shareholders (who should have been taking a close interest in their investment) but it does not threaten the money stock. This will hold as long as there are not close connections between such institutions and other institutions which do supply the means of payment.

Even so, in well-behaved banking systems problems can arise which can result in a scramble for liquidity. It is important to stress that this is a strictly domestic affair.

What can and should be done about such an occurrence? It is clear that there needs to be some agency that can supply the necessary liquidity to allay any panic. It is the function of the lender of last resort to provide liquidity to a banking system scrambling for cash. The solution is an old one and goes back to Henry Thornton at the beginning of the nineteenth century. It was set out with great clarity by Walter Bagehot before the middle of the nineteenth century, and then elaborated in *Lombard Street* (Bagehot, 1873). The banking system had undergone huge changes in the course of the century, but the solution at the end was the same as at the beginning:

> What is wanted and what is necessary to stop a panic is to diffuse the impression, that though money may be dear, still money is to be had. If people could really be convinced that they would have money, most likely they would cease to run in such a mad way for money (p. 182).

The central bank of whichever country is experiencing such a shock, resulting in a scramble for liquidity, is usually the only institution that can supply the necessary liquidity. In most cases these institutions were invested with a monopoly of note issue and when under extreme pressure would simply turn to the printing press and produce the necessary cash. It is the peculiar position of the monopoly note issuer and holder and provider of the ultimate means of payment which allows it to be the lender of last resort. Of course, this should not be done lightly. An institution with such power should use it only in extreme times, and ideally it should have established a reputation for propriety and be able to persuade the markets that the former conditions will be restored when the panic has passed.

What the central bank should not do, and indeed cannot do, is bail out an individual institution of any size. It is often argued that this is part of the function of the lender of last resort and, on occasions, that it is the only function. The reason that it cannot take such action is that it does not have sufficient capital to rescue a failing institution. In other words, a distinction can be made between the two sides of a bank's balance sheet. A shortage of liquidity is a problem for the asset side of the balance sheet; a solvency problem is a capital shortage and on the liability side.

It is often said that central banks have problems in times of crisis in terms of distinguishing between insolvency and illiquidity, and this is quite true. But the point to make is that they need not concern themselves with the distinction. If they lend freely on all good collateral that is brought to them, and if they do this anonymously, then the question need not arise.

By behaving in this way the central bank avoids another problem that is said to arise, that of moral hazard. When the term 'lender of last resort' is taken to mean the rescue of an ailing institution, the danger is that other such institutions begin to believe that they too will be saved if in difficulty. This would surely lead to more risky behaviour and higher returns since, if the price of risk is reduced, more of it will be sought. But there is little or no moral hazard involved if the institutions can simply get cash for good securities, and if they can always get it then this in itself helps to avoid panic developing. If an institution fails, it is its own fault (Capie, 2002).

There is another point to make here. Central banks have increasingly been made independent in recent times. If they have operational independence it is their job to deliver a certain price level or rate of inflation. Too much independence would not be tolerated in democratic societies, because misuse of money can have calamitous effects on the economy. If they were then in a position to bail out insolvent institutions this would mean their having to raise fresh capital – ultimately from the taxpayer. In other words, they would have taken a fiscal decision, and this should surely be outside their scope. The idea of a central bank bailing out wealthy bankers with taxpayers' money is unlikely to appeal to the electorate.

This does raise the issue of what it is the central bank is doing when it appears to come to the rescue of a (usually large) institution. There were occasions when the Bank of England organised the rescue of an institution in difficulty, usually when it felt that the failure of the institution could lead to problems in the rest of the system and perhaps a panic or crisis developing. Better, if possible, to nip such a possibility in the bud. The classic case of this is when, in 1890, the Bank was refining its skills as a lender of last resort and the institution in difficulty was Barings. Barings was overexposed in Argentina and effectively insolvent. The failure of a huge and distinguished merchant bank would probably at least have raised questions about other banks. As it happens the commercial banks were all sound. But, for whatever reason, the Bank of England organised a rescue operation. There were other occasions when similar rescues were organised. These were instances of the Bank acting as a 'crisis manager'. It ensured that a collective interest was preserved – in this case the stability of the London money markets and perhaps of London as a financial centre.

Such coordination might well have been possible without the Bank of England. At earlier points in the nineteenth century large private banks such as Rothschilds had brokered such deals. It may be that by 1890 the Bank of England had the necessary authority and reputation to render it suitable for this role. But it should be stressed that there is a clear distinction between the function of lender of last resort and that of crisis manager. The latter often does not lend at all, never mind lend in the ultimate fashion.

This clearly has implications for the possibility of an international lender of last resort. If the argument is persuasive it leads inevitably to the conclusion that there can be no international equivalent to the domestic lender of last resort. First, it is the fact that it is the ultimate issuer of the currency which allows a central bank to be the lender of last resort. Since there is no such currency beyond the national boundary, the lender's jurisdiction is limited to these national boundaries. Thus there was no international lender of last resort under the gold standard. The suggestion has on occasion been made that the Bank of England at the centre of the system and described as the 'conductor of the orchestra' was such a lender. But this is not the case. For example, if a financial crisis flared in France, this might have led to the Bank of France approaching the Bank of England directly for assistance in a normal commercial fashion, or indeed anyone else who might lend to it, but the Bank of France alone can act in France as the lender of last resort by issuing francs in sufficient quantities to quell the panic. If it followed the Bank of England practice it could do this quickly and decisively and before any gold had actually moved from elsewhere.

In the world before 1914 there were episodes that bore some resemblance to this, not necessarily involving central bank borrowing – sometimes help was organised by means of a loan brokered by a banker such as Rothschild. These arrangements were to help some countries through difficulties that threatened their ability to remain on the exchange-rate system. Similarly, in the inter-war period, stabilisation loans were made initially to help countries back to the restored gold standard. However, the system that was restored was a flawed one and further stabilisation loans were required, and organised through the League of Nations. The problem was not one of financial crisis, and no lender of last resort was involved.

The IMF's primary function was to provide temporary assistance to countries with current account imbalances. This it proceeded to do, and the system could be said to have worked more or less in this fashion, at least after the partial restoration of convertibility of currencies in 1958 and up to 1971. Even after this the loans that continued to be made right up to the 1980s were attempts to allow countries to stay on pegged exchange-rate systems. Taxpayers were generally not being called upon. But in the 1990s loans on a scale previously barely conceived of were made to countries *after* their exchange-rate regime had broken down. Worse, the scale of the loans meant there were substantial transfers from ordinary taxpayers to a wealthier group.

Even if we turn a blind eye to this violation of the basic principle of the lender of last resort – that is, that bail-outs have been carried out – we have seen that the IMF is actually incapable of coming to the rescue of many of those in difficulty. It does not have the resources. It was in fact unable to extend the necessary funds to Mexico in 1995. The only way it could have such funds would be if individual central banks ceded to it the right to issue their currencies. This, however, requires us to abandon the real world. In any case it does nothing to confront the problem of moral hazard involved in rescuing individual countries.

10 CONCLUSIONS

From this short survey of the experience of capital flows and capital controls in the world economy since around 1870, several conclusions can be drawn. Perhaps it should be stressed first that the case *for* capital flows is a simple and compelling one. Free capital movements allow individuals to reduce risk and so improve their portfolios of assets. World savings get channelled to their most productive uses. Further, the international capital markets allow countries to lend or borrow according to their circumstances and so improve their welfare.

The case against restrictions is equally clear. The first is that protection of any kind results in 'deadweight losses', and exchange controls are no exception. In Chapter 7 the discussion of British controls showed what the welfare triangles looked like. Under protectionist policies not only are prices higher and quantities lower, there are also bureaucratic and administrative costs. Some indication of their scale in the British experience was noted.

A second conclusion is suggested by consideration of the longer historical period: that once controls are introduced – for whatever reason – they do seem to take a long time to remove. Again this is like most protectionist devices. So, even if there were an argument for their imposition because of some emergency (the most convincing case being that of war), they invariably long outlast their usefulness. This was clearly demonstrated in the British case. Exchange controls were introduced in 1939 in time of war but in 1947 were firmly established in law after the war. They then remained in place until 1979. The latter part of that period was one of floating exchange rates, when it is difficult to conjure up any case at all for such controls. Therefore for some long period they were harmful and for a further period they were either harmful or redundant.

A third point is that they damage the credibility of government policy in the market environment. For example, after they had been in place in Britain for many years, they were removed in October 1979. But the Labour Party Opposition of the time continued to think in terms of reintroducing them or something akin to them, as was shown in an analysis of the proposal for a National Investment Bank in the 1980s. Credibility takes a long time to acquire, but can be destroyed quite quickly. What may be presented as a short-term emergency measure and as a one-off policy may be viewed differently in the markets.

A striking illustration of the acquisition of credibility was that achieved by the good behaviour of British governments in the eighteenth century. Borrowing on a huge scale was necessary to fight a long series of wars. Proper arrangements for repayment were made along with the introduction of new and convincing financial instruments; and regular prompt repayment developed considerable trust. In contrast the French were unable to borrow on such a scale and the fortunes of the two countries began to diverge sharply. The lesson was clear to Alexander Hamilton in the US, and in 1790, as Washington's Secretary to the Treasury, he proposed in his Report on Public Credit that the states' debts relating to the pre-revolutionary war years be paid in full.

Perhaps, though, the most important point of all to make is

the following. In peacetime, with proper exchange-rate regimes in place, there is no case for capital controls. This is first of all suggested by the experience of the nineteenth century. Capital flows then took place on a huge scale, and with the entirely credible fixed exchange-rate regime of the gold standard in place no serious problems arose. The problem arises when exchange rates are no longer credible. This was the case in the inter-war years when the gold standard was restored on an unsatisfactory basis, and the increasing political uncertainty and then instability led to capital flight and to attempts to prevent it. As Robert Mundell said in his Lionel Robbins Lectures (Mundell, 2000), it is a myth that capital flows are destructive and destabilising; there is no such thing as a bad capital movement, only bad exchange-rate systems.

The problem in the world of the last two decades or so has been similar. There have been pegged exchange rates or fixed but adjustable rates, which have not been convincing. They were almost guaranteed to produce crises. The probability of crisis rises sharply when domestic banking systems are, and are seen to be, fragile. In other words, domestic banking weakness and the lack of credibility in exchange rates constitute the problem, and it is these which should be addressed and rectified. There seems to have been a belief in the 1990s that capital controls worked, so that countries that employed them were immune to crises. The experience of Korea and Brazil exposed the weakness of this belief. Exchange controls are not the solution.

To argue that controls are needed to give such countries time to sort out their affairs – sometimes reckoned to be as much as ten years – is surely to dodge the issue. If countries are to be able to borrow on the international capital markets they must behave in such a way as to persuade lenders that they are reliable. Admittedly, reputation cannot be acquired overnight. But there is no substitute for it, as economic development so frequently and fully demonstrated in the nineteenth century.

A related element here is the role played by international institutions. The IMF has been at the centre of much recent discussion. A view emerging is that it should not arrange and support the bailouts of such errant countries. The IMF has been searching for a new role, following the short-lived experience of the Bretton Woods arrangements and the breakdown in 1971. As Larry Summers, the current US Secretary to the Treasury, argued at the London Business School in December 1999, countries should find their capital needs in the international capital market (though of course this does presuppose some sort of reputation). The IMF's activities should be heavily circumscribed, and directed to promoting improved flows of information, greater use of accepted accounting and other standards, and a highly selective financing role focused on extreme emergencies.

REFERENCES AND FURTHER READING

Aldcroft, D.H., and Oliver, M. (1998), *Exchange Rate Regimes in the Twentieth Century*, Edward Elgar, Cheltenham.

Atkin, John (1970), 'Official Regulation of British Overseas Investment, 1914–1931', *Economic History Review*, XXIII (2).

Bagehot, W. (1873), *Lombard Street: a description of the money market*, John Murray, London.

Bakker, Age F.P. (1996), *The Liberalisation of Capital Movements in Europe*, Kluwer, Dordrecht.

Bank of England (1967), 'The UK exchange control: a short history', *Quarterly Bulletin*, September.

Bank of England (1976), 'The investment currency market', *Quarterly Bulletin*, September.

Bernanke, B., and James, H. (1991), 'The gold standard, deflation, and financial crisis in the Great Depression: an international comparison', in R.G. Hubbard (ed.), *Financial Markets and Financial Crises*, Chicago University Press, Chicago, Ill.

Bhagwati, J. (1978), *Anatomy and Consequences of Exchange Control Regimes*, vol. XI, 'Foreign Trade Regimes and Economic Development', Ballinger, Cambridge, Mass.

Bloomfield, A.I. (1968), *Patterns of Fluctuation in International Investment before 1914*, Princeton Studies in International Finance, no. 21, Princeton University, Department of Economics, International Finance Section, Princeton, NJ.

Bordo, Michael (1986), 'Finance Crises, Banking Crises, Stock Market Crashes and the Money Supply: some international evidence, 1870-1933', in Capie and Wood (eds), *Financial Crises*, Macmillan, London.

Camdessus, Michel (1999), *IMF Survey*, XXVIII (23), 13 December.

Capie, Forrest (2002), 'The evolution of the lender of last resort', in P.K. O'Brien and D. Winch (eds), British Academy centennial volume.

Child, F. (1958), *The Theory and Practice of Exchange Control in Germany*, Martinus Nijhoff, The Hague.

Chown, J. (1979), 'Exchange control for ever?', *The Banker*.

Cooper, Richard (1998), *Should Capital Account Convertibility Be a World Objective?*, Princeton Studies in International Finance, no. 207, Princeton University, Department of Economics, International Finance Section, Princeton, NJ.

Day, John (1987), *The Medieval Market Economy*, Blackwell, Oxford.

de la Cuadra, S., and Valdes, S. (1992), 'Myths and facts about financial liberalisation in Chile, 1974– 83', in P. Brock (ed.), *If Texas Were Chile: A Primer on Banking Reform*, ICS Press, San Francisco, Calif., pp. 11–101.

Demsetz, Harold (1969), 'Information and efficiency: another viewpoint', *Journal of Law and Economics*, XII (1).

Eatwell, John (1996), *International Financial Liberalisation. The Impact on World Development*, United Nations Development Programme, Office of Development Studies, New York, NY.

Edwards, Jeremy, and Fischer, Klaus (1994), *Banks, Finance and Investment in Germany*, Cambridge University Press, Cambridge.

Edwards, Sebastian (1999a), 'On crisis prevention: lessons from

Mexico and East Asia', www.anderson.ucla.edu/faculty/
    sebastian.edwards/, June.

Edwards, Sebastian (1999b), 'How effective are capital controls?',
    Journal of Economic Perspectives, XIII (4).

Eichengreen, B. (1998), 'Trends and cycles in foreign lending', in
    Horst Siebert (ed.), *Capital Flows in the World Economy*, Mohr,
    Tübingen.

Einzig, P. (1934), *Exchange Control*, Macmillan, London.

Ellis, H. (1941), *Exchange Control in Germany*, Cambridge
    University Press, Cambridge.

Feinstein, Charles, and Watson, Katherine (1995), 'Private
    international capital flows in Europe in the interwar period',
    in Feinstein (ed.), *Banking, Currency and Finance in Europe
    between the Wars*, Clarendon Press, Oxford.

Feldstein, M. (1993), 'Lesson of the Bretton Woods experience', in
    M. Bordo and B. Eichengreen (eds), *A Retrospective on the
    Bretton Woods System*, NBER/University of Chicago Press,
    Chicago, Ill.

Fforde, John (1992), *The Bank of England and Public Policy*,
    Cambridge University Press, Cambridge.

Friedman, Milton (1953), 'The case for flexible exchange rates', in
    Essays in Positive Economics, University of Chicago Press,
    Chicago, Ill.

Haberler, Gottfried (1939), *Prosperity and Depression*, League of
    Nations, Geneva.

Hayek, F.A. (1944), *The Road to Serfdom*, Routledge & Kegan Paul,
    London.

Howson, S. (1980), 'The management of sterling 1932–39', *Journal
    of Economic History*, XL (1).

James, Harold (1992), 'Financial flows across frontiers', *Economic

History Review, XLV (3).

James, Harold (2003), 'From exchange and banking control to convertibility and floating exchange rates', in *Towards a Global System*, forthcoming.

Kindleberger, C. (1984), *A Financial History of Western Europe*, George Allen & Unwin, London.

Kitson, M., and Solomou, S. (1998), *Bilateralism in the Interwar World Economy*, Working Paper 9101, Department of Applied Economics, Cambridge.

Klug, Adam (1993), *The German Buybacks, 1932–1939: a cure for overhang*, Princeton Studies in International Finance, Princeton University, Department of Economics, International Finance Section, Princeton, NJ.

League of Nations (1937), *Money and Banking*, Geneva.

League of Nations (1938), *Report on Exchange Control*, Geneva.

McKinnon, R. (1993), 'The origins of the fixed rate dollar standard: Bretton Woods or the Marshall Plan', in M. Bordo and B. Eichengreen (eds), *A Retrospective on the Bretton Woods System*, NBER/University of Chicago Press, Chicago, Ill.

Michie, Ranald (1999), *The London Stock Exchange: A History*, Oxford University Press, Oxford.

Miller, Robert, and Wood, John (1979), *Exchange Control for Ever?*, Research Monograph no. 33, Institute for Economic Affairs, London.

Mitchell, B.R. (1998), *International Historical Statistics: Europe 1750–1993*, 4th ed., Macmillan, London.

Mundell, R. (1963), 'Capital mobility and stabilisation policy under fixed and flexible exchange rates', *Canadian Journal of Economics*, XXIX.

Mundell, R. (1993), 'An agreement not a system', in M. Bordo and

B. Eichengreen (eds), *A Retrospective on the Bretton Woods System*, NBER/University of Chicago Press, Chicago, Ill.

Mundell, R. (2000), 'A reinterpretation of the twentieth century', Lionel Robbins Lectures, London School of Economics, January.

Neal, Larry (1979), 'The economics and finance of bilateral clearing agreements: Germany, 1934–8', *Economic History Review*, XXXII (3).

Neal, Larry (1990), *The Rise of Financial Capitalism*, Cambridge University Press, Cambridge.

Nurkse, Ragnar (1944), *Interwar Currency Experience*, League of Nations, Geneva.

Obstfeld, M., and Rogoff, K. (1996), *Foundations of International Finance*, MIT Press, Boston, Mass.

Obstfeld, Maurice, and Taylor, Alan M. (1998), 'The great depression as a watershed: international capital mobility over the long run', in M. Bordo, C. Goldin, E.N. White (eds), *The Defining Moment: The Great Depression and the American Economy in the Twentieth Century*, Chicago University Press, Chicago, Ill.

Pepper, Gordon T., and Oliver, Michael J. (2001), *Monetarism Under Thatcher: Lessons for the Future*, Edward Elgar, Cheltenham.

Phylaktis, Kate, and Wood, Geoffrey E. (1984), 'An analytical and taxonomic framework for the study of exchange controls', in J. Black and G. Dorrance (eds), *Problems of International Finance*, Macmillan, London.

Pressnell, L.S. (1986), *External Economic Policy since the War*, HMSO, London.

Pressnell, L.S. (1997), 'What went wrong? The evolution of the IMF 1941–1961', *Banca Nazionale del Lavoro Quarterly Review*, no. 201.

Reddaway, W.B. (1968), *Effects of UK Direct Investments Overseas*, Cambridge University Press, Cambridge.

Redish, Angela (1993), 'Anchors aweigh: the transition from commodity money to fiat money in western economies', *Canadian Journal of Economics*, XXVI (4).

Ritschl, A. (2001), 'Nazi economic imperialism and the exploitation of the small', *Economic History Review*, L11 (2).

Robertson, D.H. (1954), *Britain in the World Economy*, George Allen & Unwin, London.

Sayers, R.S. (1976), *The Bank of England, 1891–1944*, Cambridge University Press, Cambridge.

Stigler, George J. (1994), 'Imperfections in the Capital Market', in Mervyn Lewis (ed.), *Financial Intermediaries*, pp. 241–6, Edward Elgar, Cheltenham.

Suzuki, Toshio (1993), *Japanese Government Loan Issues on the London Capital Market 1870–1913*, Athlone Press, London.

Tobin, James (1978), 'A proposal for international monetary reform', *Eastern Economic Journal*, 4: 153–9.

United Nations, Department of Economics Affairs (1949), *International Capital Movements during the Inter-War Period*, Lake Success, NY.

United Nations, Department of Economic and Social Affairs (1959), *The International Flow of Private Capital, 1956–1958*, Lake Success, NY.

Wright, J.F. (1997), 'The Contribution of Overseas Savings to the Funded National Debt in Great Britain', *Economic History Review*, L (3).

Wyplosz, Charles (1999), 'Financial restraints on liberalization in postwar Europe', www.unige.ch/~wyplosz/, January.

ABOUT THE IEA

The Institute is a research and educational charity (No. CC 235 351), limited by guarantee. Its mission is to improve understanding of the fundamental institutions of a free society with particular reference to the role of markets in solving economic and social problems.

The IEA achieves its mission by:

- a high-quality publishing programme
- conferences, seminars, lectures and other events
- outreach to school and college students
- brokering media introductions and appearances

The IEA, which was established in 1955 by the late Sir Antony Fisher, is an educational charity, not a political organisation. It is independent of any political party or group and does not carry on activities intended to affect support for any political party or candidate in any election or referendum, or at any other time. It is financed by sales of publications, conference fees and voluntary donations.

In addition to its main series of publications the IEA also publishes a quarterly journal, *Economic Affairs*, and has two specialist programmes – Environment and Technology, and Education.

The IEA is aided in its work by a distinguished international Academic Advisory Council and an eminent panel of Honorary Fellows. Together with other academics, they review prospective IEA publications, their comments being passed on anonymously to authors. All IEA papers are therefore subject to the same rigorous independent refereeing process as used by leading academic journals.

IEA publications enjoy widespread classroom use and course adoptions in schools and universities. They are also sold throughout the world and often translated/reprinted.

Since 1974 the IEA has helped to create a world-wide network of 100 similar institutions in over 70 countries. They are all independent but share the IEA's mission.

Views expressed in the IEA's publications are those of the authors, not those of the Institute (which has no corporate view), its Managing Trustees, Academic Advisory Council members or senior staff.

Members of the Institute's Academic Advisory Council, Honorary Fellows, Trustees and Staff are listed on the following page.

The Institute gratefully acknowledges financial support for its publications programme and other work from a generous benefaction by the late Alec and Beryl Warren.

111

Other papers recently published by the IEA include:

WHO, What and Why?

Transnational Government, Legitimacy and the World Health Organization
Roger Scruton
Occasional Paper 113; ISBN 0 255 36487 3
£8.00

The World Turned Rightside Up

A New Trading Agenda for the Age of Globalisation
John C. Hulsman
Occasional Paper 114; ISBN 0 255 36495 4
£8.00

The Representation of Business in English Literature

Introduced and edited by Arthur Pollard
Readings 53; ISBN 0 255 36491 1
£12.00

Anti-Liberalism 2000

The Rise of New Millennium Collectivism
David Henderson
Occasional Paper 115; ISBN 0 255 36497 0
£7.50

Capitalism, Morality and Markets

Brian Griffiths, Robert A. Sirico, Norman Barry & Frank Field
Readings 54; ISBN 0 255 36496 2
£7.50

A Conversation with Harris and Seldon

Ralph Harris & Arthur Seldon
Occasional Paper 116; ISBN 0 255 36498 9
£7.50

Malaria and the DDT Story

Richard Tren & Roger Bate
Occasional Paper 117; ISBN 0 255 36499 7
£10.00

A Plea to Economists Who Favour Liberty: Assist the Everyman

Daniel B. Klein
Occasional Paper 118; ISBN 0 255 36501 2
£10.00

Waging the War of Ideas

John Blundell

Occasional Paper 119; ISBN 0 255 36500 4

£10.00

The Changing Fortunes of Economic Liberalism

Yesterday, Today and Tomorrow

David Henderson

Occasional Paper 105 (new edition); ISBN 0 255 36520 9

£12.50

The Global Education Industry

Lessons from Private Education in Developing Countries

James Tooley

Hobart Paper 141 (new edition); ISBN 0 255 36503 9

£12.50

Saving Our Streams

*The Role of the Anglers' Conservation Association in
Protecting English and Welsh Rivers*

Roger Bate

Research Monograph 53; ISBN 0 255 36494 6

£10.00

Better Off Out?
The Benefits or Costs of EU Membership
Brian Hindley & Martin Howe
Occasional Paper 99 (new edition); ISBN 0 255 36502 0
£10.00

Buckingham at 25
Freeing the Universities from State Control
Edited by James Tooley
Readings 55; ISBN 0 255 36512 8
£15.00

Lectures on Regulatory and Competition Policy
Irwin M. Stelzer
Occasional Paper 120; ISBN 0 255 36511 X
£12.50

Misguided Virtue
False Notions of Corporate Social Responsibility
David Henderson
Hobart Paper 142; ISBN 0 255 36510 1
£12.50

HIV and Aids in Schools

The Political Economy of Pressure Groups and Miseducation
Barrie Craven, Pauline Dixon, Gordon Stewart & James Tooley
Occasional Paper 121; ISBN 0 255 36522 5
£10.00

The Road to Serfdom

The Reader's Digest *condensed version*
Friedrich A. Hayek
Occasional Paper 122; ISBN 0 255 36530 6
£7.50

Bastiat's *The Law*

Introduction by Norman Barry
Occasional Paper 123; ISBN 0 255 36509 8
£7.50

A Globalist Manifesto for Public Policy

Charles Calomiris
Occasional Paper 124; ISBN 0 255 36525 X
£7.50

Euthanasia for Death Duties

Putting Inheritance Tax Out of Its Misery
Barry Bracewell-Milnes
Research Monograph 54; ISBN 0 255 36513 6
£10.00

Liberating the Land

The Case for Private Land-use Planning
Mark Pennington
Hobart Paper 143; ISBN 0 255 36508 x
£10.00

IEA Yearbook of Government Performance 2002/2003

Edited by Peter Warburton
Yearbook 1; ISBN 0 255 36532 2
£15.00

Britain's Relative Economic Performance, 1870–1999

Nicholas Crafts
Research Monograph 55; ISBN 0 255 36524 1
£10.00

Should We Have Faith in Central Banks?

Otmar Issing

Occasional Paper 125; ISBN 0 255 36528 4

£7.50

The Dilemma of Democracy

The Political Economics of Over-government

Arthur Seldon

Hobart Paper 136 (reissue); ISBN 0 255 36536 5

£10.00

To order copies of currently available IEA papers, or to enquire about availability, please contact:

Lavis Marketing
73 Lime Walk
Oxford OX3 7AD

Tel: 01865 767575
Fax: 01865 750079
Email: orders@lavismarketing.co.uk

The IEA also offers a subscription service to its publications. For a single annual payment, currently £40.00 in the UK, you will receive every title the IEA publishes across the course of a year, invitations to events, and discounts on our extensive back catalogue. For more information, please contact:

Subscriptions
The Institute of Economic Affairs
2 Lord North Street
London SW1P 3LB

Tel: 020 7799 8900
Fax: 020 7799 2137
Website: www.iea.org.uk